teach yourself®

P9-DGO-083

travel writing

travel writing
cynthia dial

For over 60 years, more than 40 million people have learnt over 750 subjects the **teach yourself** way, with impressive results.

be where you want to be
with **teach yourself**

For UK order enquiries: please contact Bookpoint Ltd., 130 Milton Park, Abingdon, Oxon OX14 4SB. Telephone: +44 (0) 1235 827720. Fax: +44 (0) 1235 400454. Lines are open 09.00–17.00, Monday to Saturday, with a 24-hour message answering service. Details about our titles and how to order are available at www.teachyourself.co.uk

For USA order enquiries: please contact McGraw-Hill Customer Services, PO Box 545, Blacklick, OH 43004-0545, USA. Telephone: 1-800-722-4726. Fax: 1-614-755-5645.

For Canada order enquiries: please contact McGraw-Hill Ryerson Ltd., 300 Water St, Whitby, Ontario L1N 9B6, Canada. Telephone: 905 430 5000. Fax: 905 430 5020.

Long renowned as the authoritative source for self-guided learning – with more than 40 million copies sold worldwide – the **teach yourself** series includes over 300 titles in the fields of languages, crafts, hobbies, business, computing and education.

British Library Cataloguing in Publication Data: a catalogue record for this title is available from The British Library.

Library of Congress Catalog Card Number: on file

First published in UK 2001 by Hodder Education, 338 Euston Road, London, NW1 3BH.

First published in US 2001 by The McGraw-Hill Companies, Inc.

This edition published 2003.

The **teach yourself** name is a registered trade mark of Hodder Headline.

Copyright © 2001, 2003 Cynthia W. Dial

In UK: All rights reserved. Apart from any permitted use under UK copyright law, no part of this publication may be reproduced or transmitted in any form or by any means, electronic or mechanical, including photocopy, recording, or any information, storage and retrieval system, without permission in writing from the publisher or under licence from the Copyright Licensing Agency Limited. Further details of such licences (for reprographic reproduction) may be obtained from the Copyright Licensing Agency Limited, of 90 Tottenham Court Road, London, W1T 4LP.

In US: All rights reserved. Except as permitted under the United States Copyright Act of 1976, no part of this publication may be reproduced or distributed in any form or by any means, or stored in a database or retrieval system, without the prior written permission of the publisher.

Typeset by Transet Limited, Coventry, England.
Printed in Great Britain for Hodder Education, a division of Hodder Headline, 338 Euston Road, London, NW1 3BH by Cox & Wyman Ltd., Reading, Berkshire.

Hodder Headline's policy is to use papers that are natural, renewable and recyclable products and made from wood grown in sustainable forests. The logging and manufacturing processes are expected to conform to the environmental regulations of the country of origin.

Impression number   10 9 8 7 6 5 4 3
Year   2007 2006

v

contents

Cynthia Dial has been a travel writer since 1988. Her entry into the profession was rather roundabout. It was the result of a career change from writing and producing audio-visual films in Chicago to entering the travel industry in San Diego. After several years of loving travel but missing writing, she combined the two. Thus, her travel writing career was born. Since that time, she has published hundreds of travel articles in national and international newspapers and magazines. For over five years she contributed approximately 24 articles a year as a contributing editor to two leading industry magazines. In addition, her work has appeared in a variety of travel and special interest publications, ranging from Radisson International's *Voyageur* magazine to the bilingual in-flight magazine *Aboard*. Her travel specialties include golf, spas, soft adventure and upscale travel destinations and activities.

This book is based on a travel writing course entitled *Travel Writing: For Those Who Love to Travel and Long to Write About It* that she teaches in the Southern California area for aspiring travel writers of all ages and abilities. She also guest lectures at national forums such as Whidbey Island Writers' Conference in the Seattle, Washington, area and the Southern California Writers' Conference. She holds a Bachelor of Journalism degree from the University of Texas at Austin as well as a CTC (Certified Travel Counselor) travel industry certification.

She lives in San Diego, California, with her husband, Kent, and enjoys time with their recently-graduated university student daughters, Erin and Kathryn. The rest of the time she travels.

introduction

One of the primary benefits of my career as a travel writer is the opportunity to travel – and to travel a lot. It always amazes me when my extensive travel experience creates something of a semi-celebrity status. The result is that at parties or even children's soccer games I've been cornered by mere acquaintances in quest of the inside track on New Zealand, or India or wherever.

As a travel writer you will become trained – trained not only to experience a destination fully – but also to become well versed in that area. You'll become a travel expert; you'll come to know the options for getting into Bangkok from the airport, if a car is a necessity or a burden in San Francisco and that a *pousada* is a unique alternative to a hotel in Portugal.

And it's this reservoir of knowledge, accumulated over years of travel, that you, the writer, will share – from the most in-depth observation to the tiniest tidbit – in a newspaper article, a piece in a travel magazine or the pages of a book.

If you have a sincere desire to impart your insight through the written word, however, certain steps must be taken. Travel writing can, indeed, turn travels into saleable copy, but writing an effective article is not as easy as reiterating pages from a detailed travel journal.

The purpose of this book is to simplify the process for the aspiring travel writer, noting the essential steps to take and pointing out possible pitfalls. In short, my goal is to give you the tools necessary to put your travel experiences on paper and sell them.

On the surface, my entry into the travel writing arena appears to have been simple. During my stint as a travel agent, a new travel industry magazine crossed my desk. The magazine, *Travel People* (which has since ceased publication), showcased those working in the travel industry in non-traditional roles. One of the first issues featured Kitty Dukakis (wife of politician Michael Dukakis and first lady of Massachusetts), who at that time worked in travel.

Through my affiliation in the local San Diego travel community I had become acquainted with Billy Riley, a colourful 70-year-old Southern belle who was general manager of a new property, the Horton Grand Hotel. Comprised of two century-old hotels disassembled brick by brick, reconstructed side by side and restored with loving care, the property became one of the city's historic landmarks. And under the diligence of Miss Billy (as she was affectionately called), who sashayed throughout the antique-strewn hotel in a period dress with a matching bonnet while graciously setting the stage for the past, the property thrived.

As I came to know Miss Billy, I became as impressed with her past accomplishments as I was with her present endeavours. I learned she was quite a trailblazer for local female hotel executives, having been San Diego's first female general manager of a major hotel, first female president of the hotel/motel association and first female recipient of the city's annual Travel Industry Person-of-the-Year award.

Seeing the potential of a story in Miss Billy, I wrote a query letter to the editor of *Travel People* stating my case. I complimented her on the new publication and the recent piece on Massachusetts' first lady. Continuing I stated that San Diego also had a 'first lady', Miss Billy Riley (citing her travel industry firsts), and that I would like to tell the publication's readers about this distinctive, accomplished individual.

Shortly afterwards, I received a go-ahead from the editor. I interviewed Miss Billy, shot several rolls of film and wrote a 1000-word piece, which was sent in a timely manner. In return, I received a cheque and a copy of the article with my byline. My first query and my first draft resulted in my first cheque and clip. For me, this career was exceedingly easy. Right? Wrong.

The next month I was invited to visit a country as a VIP guest during a period when safety was a concern in some of its regions. I've since joked that my only consolation as the mother of two young children was my belief that my husband would be a good single parent. My travel experience, however, was a priceless visit during which time I never felt unsafe.

Upon returning, I sent a query letter to a varity of major US newspapers. Continuing with my perceived good luck, I received the reply 'Yes, on spec' (on speculation) from *The Dallas Morning News*, *The Los Angeles Times* and *The San Francisco Examiner*. Naively, I had already begun to rest on my laurels and assumed my luck would prevail.

The resulting article, which was sent to each of the three newspapers, was good. But even I knew it wasn't great. I received three rejections. Was I devastated? Yes. Was I humbled? A resounding yes. Was I discouraged? You bet. But did I learn anything? Absolutely.

I learned that the roller-coaster career of a travel writer is replete with ups and downs. My new goal, in addition to being published, became maximizing the ups and minimizing the downs. And it's that insight I share with you, the aspiring travel writer, in the following pages.

01

I'm a travel writer: welcome to my life

Let me describe one of my work days. I lazily lie in a hammock securely strung between two palms, swaying back and forth, back and forth. My eyes focus towards the cloudless cobalt sky. It is late afternoon. I'm luxuriating in the moment, making note of everything – the gentle sea breeze, the pearlized sand and the hypnotic roll of the surf. I'm in Fiji, I'm recollecting every detail of my morning and I'm working. The day started with a village tour and a catamaran cruise to an uninhabited island, complete with an outdoor barbecue, snorkelling and impromptu dancing to the beat of a native band. Tonight I'm the resort's guest at its weekly *meke* (Fijian-style *luau*). Tomorrow it's on to Tonga where I'll attend Sunday service at the local church – I've been told to expect to see His Majesty King Taufa'ahau Tupou IV, a member of the congregation. My only complaint of this work day? I still have to pack and I should have used more sunscreen.

But to illustrate the complete picture of a travel writer's life fairly, I'll briefly recap one more day. Indulge me as this description is crucial to consider before you gather your suitcase, notebook and camera in quest of your newly acclaimed travel writing career.

Surrounded by pamphlets, maps, press kits, notes and slides, I sit at my desk and stare at a blank computer screen. I'm on deadline. I spent my morning on the Internet, checking and double-checking facts and making a time-consuming, yet fruitless search for an important detail. A brusque, not-so-friendly editor phoned and explained that he likes my recently submitted piece but needs an additional 500-word sidebar within two days. And the school just called. My daughter has an ear infection.

Now that I have your attention and your luggage is back in the closet, let's talk reality. To be a successful (**definition**: one who is published and will be invited to visit destinations like Fiji and Tonga) travel writer, you play many roles. One obvious role is that of a reporter; others include historian, grammarian, private investigator, photographer and diplomat. And for some stories, you'll become a shopper, skier, hiker, theatre-goer or diner. Remember, the list is full but it is far from complete. The requisites change from piece to piece, publication to publication and year to year.

Travel writer traits

What separates the traveller from the travel writer? There are a number of key characteristics found in journalists whose beat, you might say, is the world. Travel writers come in assorted shapes and sizes. They fall into job categories ranging from full-time staff positions to part-time freelancing. While this book is designed to impart valuable information to any travel journalist, it is written with the freelancer in mind. Following (in no particular order) is an inventory of helpful character traits:

Creative: Helps you unearth an unusual angle that captures an editor's eye, and to write prose that sparkles when you sit down at the computer, typewriter or with your notebook.

Resourceful: When searching for hard-to-find details or trying to orchestrate an interview with an evasive camel jockey for a Giza pyramid piece, you must rely on this trait.

Energetic: You'll alternate between difficult travel schedules and demanding deadlines.

Self-motivated: You're your own boss if you freelance and your office is frequently your home. This set-up creates a daily temptation – procrastination.

Flexible: You must continually juggle between writing, research, contacting editors, extensive travel and even packing. It's a hassle, but it's your way of life.

Competitive: The competition among travel writers is keen, keener than any writing genre. It is imperative to stand out, to be a cut above the others and, in the end, receive those coveted assignments.

Organized: You face multiple tasks – you travel to a variety of countries, approach innumerable editors and write an assortment of pieces. The answer is organization.

Goal oriented: Your aim is to get your name in print, as often as possible, and to get paid for it. This objective requires constant focus.

Healthy: Travel is never easy on the body. Combine the endless hours in route with toting heavy camera equipment and being on duty the minute you arrive in a locale. The result is a mixture with one indispensable ingredient – good health.

Skilful: Good writing is key to getting published.

Adventurous: To capture the elements of some stories, you must be willing to experience things you've never tried before.

Inquisitive: You seek the unique, explore the unknown, continually ask yourself questions and find the answers.

Determined: Tracking down crucial elements, sometimes in the face of resistance and many times in a foreign country, demands tenacity. You must persevere to discover the exotic and the extraordinary, as well as to note the simple and basic.

People oriented: People eagerly share their towns, their countries and, in some cases, their homes to help acquaint you with their cultures. Encourage this interaction.

Trustworthy: Reporting about occurrences on the opposite side of the world, as well as around the corner, carries its responsibilities. Remember, you share the world's secrets.

Positive: A quality you'll find essential in many travel writing scenarios like delving through reams and reams of material to double-check one small fact, dealing with a cancelled flight or staying in accommodation with no running water.

Broadminded: Customs, cultures, religions and people of other lands are, by virtue of the definition of the word *foreign,* different. You must respect those differences.

Curious: Who, what, when, where and why are questions you strive to answer.

Creditable: This characteristic is double-fold. You must represent the travel experience honestly – for the host country, hotel, restaurant, etc., as well as for your readers.

Independent: You eat many meals alone, visit some of the world's most romantic haunts solo and explore third world countries with no cohort.

The final characteristic is certainly not one I or most travel writers possess. It is included, however, to add a bit of humour, as well as a touch of reality to this already lengthy list.

Independently wealthy: Fringe benefits translate into big money for you. However, the pay most likely will not.

You're not a tourist, you're a writer

As a travel writer, you're no longer a tourist – you must absorb surroundings, note details, contrast and compare – whether it be a resort, an airline, a village, even a country. You're inherently observant and must put these observations into text – honestly, interestingly and accurately. And as a professional journalist, you're as hungry to report the nuts and bolts of your travel revelations as you are its romantic and intriguing aspects.

If you love it, you can learn it

To be a *published* travel writer, however, you must be able to write. It's been said that writing cannot be taught – it can only be learned. From my experience on the teaching circuit, I have come to conclude that an interest in writing is coupled with an ability to write, however latent that ability might be. Like getting to an onion's core, writing talent may be suppressed under layer upon layer of doubt. This 'I can't write' spirit may have been fuelled by years of subtle negativity. But my motto is: If you love it, you can learn it. Writing is no exception.

To break through this barrier, I prescribe attending classes, devouring books with titles like *Write Right!* and *100 Ways to Improve Your Writing* and ferociously pursuing the written word, as an observer and a participant. If I were to make one assignment to the would-be travel writer, it would be the same advice I received in an introductory writing class: 'Analyze and imitate.'

Analyze and imitate

Read newspaper travel sections and magazine travel pieces, no longer for information alone, but for style as well. As expected, articles in *Travel & Leisure* and *Conde Nast Traveler British Edition* are strong examples of good writing in this genre. But study travel articles in any and all publications. They're everywhere – in bridal, family, women's, men's, in-flight, health, senior, trade and association magazines.

Examine travel writing. Carefully ask yourself what makes an article good enough to read every paragraph and thirst for more. Pay attention to titles. Become a student of a travel article's lead (the opening sentence). Scrutinize the article – what was most informative, most helpful. Notice styles.

If you read ten good articles on the same destination by an equal number of authors, there will be ten different approaches and a like number of styles – all good but all *different*. Analyze these articles. Imitate these articles. This is not a permit for plagiarism. Simply familiarize yourself with what works. Collect *irresistible* travel pieces. Note why they're irresistible.

After reading innumerable travel articles that work, on a variety of subjects of interest, it's almost through osmosis that good writing becomes ingrained in the would-be writer.

Study non-fiction and fiction

Preparation through reading does not stop with travel articles. Study good fiction and soak up its creativity. Non-fiction can be as creative as fiction. Well-written non-fiction goes beyond the who, what, when, where and why to *show what it was like*. Note how to use fiction techniques in your non-fiction to draw the reader into the action – action that is fascinating because it is factual, and forceful because it is personal.

Read a variety of fiction. I enjoy Sue Grafton's alphabet mystery books for their simplicity. I read Michael Crichton's work for his vivid descriptions and expert storytelling.

Reading fiction is one of my favourite forms of research. This is the research I employ at times when I'm creatively depleted. While I may not be producing verbiage on these days, I *am* becoming a better writer.

When in the throes of seeking your own style, you may fear your personal style will be influenced by another writer. The definitive answer is that it *will* be influenced and it *won't* be influenced. Have no fear your prose will be mistaken for Hemingway's. Yet strive to recreate a scene as succulently descriptive as this passage from the famed author's work, *The Snows of Kilimanjaro*.

> *That was where they walked up the sleigh-smoothed urine-*
> *yellowed road along the river with the steep pine hills, skis*
> *heavy on the shoulder, and where they ran that great run*

*down the glacier above the Madlener-haus, the snow as
smooth to see as cake frosting and as light as powder and
he remembered the noiseless rush the speed made as you
dropped down like a bird.*

Rest assured of one thing. Your individual mode of expression
will not be compromised. Personal writing style is as unique and
distinct as your fingerprints. The key to developing a good,
compelling one is to work and to work hard at it, then hone it
and fine tune it.

Analyzing bad travel articles is as important as imitating good
ones. Assume the role of an editor and assess a travel story.
Don't simply toss a piece aside because you've deemed it *bad*
writing. The value of an unappealing piece is in the answers to
an assortment of questions. Why doesn't it work? Is it boring?
Does it not inform? Is it too flowery? Are the descriptions flat?
How does it flow? Make another travel writer's poor attempt at
writing work for you.

In conjunction with classes, read how-to books on writing,
creativity, grammar and travel writing, among others. Study
these books thoroughly, highlight them. Use them like college
textbooks, referring to them often.

Why write?

As exhausting as travel can be, writing, whether perched at the
keys of a state-of-the-art computer or curled in an overstuffed
chair, is one of the most draining experiences imaginable.

*Writing is the hardest work in the world not involving
heavy lifting.*

Pete Hamill

*An absolutely necessary part of a writer's equipment,
almost as necessary as talent, is the ability to stand up
under punishment, both the punishment the world hands
out and the punishment he inflicts upon himself.*

Irwin Shaw

So why do it?

You're a salesperson and the world is your territory

In a six-month period of my travel writing life, I watched the sun rise from Diamond Head during the Christmas holidays, cruised the River Nile the following month, visited a Macau gambling casino in February and explored Kauai from a helicopter the beginning of May. However, in April I was preparing for a tax audit – an example of this career's ups and downs.

International discoveries

I have experienced a *tuk-tuk* (Thailand's version of the golf cart) ride throughout the maze of Bangkok's streets. Also while in Thailand and as a measure of respect, I carefully dodged any chance of physical contact with Buddhist monks because their custom, albeit a time-consuming one, is to cleanse themselves ritualistically after even brushing against a female.

And after visiting Fiji, I incorporated the term *bula*, the island's standard greeting, into my international vocabulary. These examples are only a sampling of the world's diverse practices I've discovered while working.

Licence to ask questions

Several years ago I was sent to Egypt during terrorist activities to report whether the country was a safe destination. This piece was for a US travel trade publication geared to travel agents.

Because I was on assignment and had questions to be answered, I began working in flight, eagerly soliciting a variety of opinions. My seatmate, a tour operator, had dual (Egyptian/US) citizenship. He informed me of a fact crucial to my piece: up until that point, terrorist activity had been confined to middle Egypt (an area seldom visited by the American traveller) and away from top tourist spots such as Luxor, Valley of the Kings and the pyramids. Considering my readers, that information was paramount.

Before landing in Cairo, my interview subjects included a passenger affiliated with the Library of Congress (part of a US congressional delegation to Egypt), as well as a former brigadier general for the Egyptian Army. Asking potentially sensitive questions and approaching contacts of this calibre were not intimidating – I was doing my job.

A pad and pencil are your entry

Your credential as a travel writer literally and figuratively opens doors closed to most, even the most seasoned travel veteran. These doors can range from a new musical's stage door to the door of a hotel executive's private office.

Worldwide sense of belonging

The same travel writing credential gives you a worldwide sense of belonging when caught in one of those typically awkward travel situations, like being the sole woman in a Greek taverna or the only American at Hiroshima's Memorial Shrine. On many occasions I am the only female, the only Caucasian or the only English speaker in a setting. But do I feel conspicuous? No, because I'm on assignment.

You notice, take notes, conduct informal interviews. Get on the inside. It's important to go behind the scenes because your job is to take readers there, transport them to an unknown setting and share your collection of tidbits only locals might know.

My husband and I have spent the night in a Greek villa with a couple we met during a café dinner and I've interviewed an Egyptian waiter while perched at a counter in a bustling restaurant kitchen. Both contacts not only jettisoned me into the destination but also became a part of my global network of friends.

You observe a destination differently

It is through careful inspection and detailed dissection that you, the travel writer, view the world. While you're not an investigative reporter per se, details must be noticed and noted.

During a Diamond Head climb I made mental and physical notes of the 360° view, the number of steps climbed (a series of 69 followed by another 94) and how many unlit tunnels were traversed to reach that view. Through my eyes as a travel writer, Oahu is not simply an island paradise with turquoise water, white beaches and green palms, it is a destination to be explored studiously.

You see, smell, hear, taste and touch a destination

You use every one of your five senses when reiterating a travel episode. Describing my stay at a *pousada* in the quaint Portuguese town of Estremoz, I wrote about the morning scene that greeted me from the window ... roosters crowing at daybreak, the gentle autumn breeze fluttering through my hair and caressing my face, the tapping of children's shoes meeting the weathered cobblestones as they scurried to the local schoolhouse, the intoxicating aroma of freshly baked goods and the red-tiled rooftops below our castle fortress. Your job is to be not only your readers' eyes and ears, but their sense of taste, touch and smell as well.

> *Nothing is sillier than the creative writing teacher's dictum 'Write about what you know.' ... Preliminary good advice might be: Write as if you were a movie camera.*
>
> John Gardner

Draw on a lifetime of experiences

Any travel experience can be of value to you as a travel writer. The result of my short rainy weekend in New York, after flying all night from California's West Coast, resulted in a piece entitled 'Seeing New York from Under an Umbrella'.

Before my travel writing days, I might have summarily categorized those 48 hours as wet and wasted rather than productive and profitable. Similarly, a pickpocket in the famous Guatemalan market of Chichicastenango took approximately US $30, a couple of blank cheques and my credit card from me; but, in the process, gave me the slant for a travel article – 'Guatemala: Travel Smart/Travel Safe'.

It's all research. I visited Australia years before my travel writing career began. And yet I have repeatedly drawn upon my observations of the Sydney Opera House in my work, particularly when I describe my home town, San Diego, and its bayside, sail-inspired convention centre as reminiscent of the noted Australian landmark.

You'll write from a lifetime of background material. Whether it's the way the mud-coloured sand curled between your toes during childhood visits to the beach or the smell of chicken frying in your grandmother's heavy black iron skillet. These memories are of infinite value. Recalling personal experience breathes life into articles. It brings priceless energy to them. And it may transport your readers to their own nostalgic pasts.

Constant learning experience

In order to be taken seriously, you must appear professional. And the appearance of professionalism is best accomplished by speaking and understanding the lingo, sending the article in the correct manuscript format, presenting grammatically correct articles, etc. The list is endless.

The best preparation is obviously acquired through experience. Experience, however, is a very time-consuming process – a process that may take years. Do not despair. Acceleration of this learning curve is possible and can be reduced from a matter of years to months, weeks, even a day-long seminar. How, you might ask. Classes – classes in English, grammar, geography, general writing and, of course, travel writing.

I continue to take classes. Even though I have worked as a travel writer and taught this writing genre for the past decade, I attend classes on travel journalism and read every travel writing book I discover. Classes in grammar and creative writing, as well as lectures on countries I have visited or plan to visit, are always of interest to me. Life as a travel writer is life in a constant learning mode.

And don't overlook the value of writing workshops and conferences, where you have the opportunity to meet other writers, editors and agents; and subjects like 'How to Write for the Web' and 'Composing an Irresistible Query' are typically addressed. Even though sessions exclusively geared to travel writing are not always offered, these forums are nevertheless valuable.

Do, however, resist the urge to become a professional attendee, thinking one more workshop or conference will magically transform you into a writer. Only writing will transform you into a writer.

Keep abreast of trends

The world's best education is travel, they say. This adage is never truer than for you, the travel writer, because in order to acquaint readers with a possibly alien subject, you must learn as much about that subject as possible.

Know if Thailand's baht is falling. A currency devaluation translates to good travel bargains for your readers. The 2000 Summer Olympic Games staged in Sydney increased interest in this southern hemisphere continent. After the release of movies like *Out of Africa*, *Sleepless in Seattle* and *Notting Hill*, these destinations' universal appeal increased dramatically. If an area becomes fashionable, capitalize on its new-found popularity.

Are an abundance of women's magazines addressing females travelling alone? If so, consider articles like 'Travel Safely, Travel Wisely' or 'London's Top 10 Restaurants for a Solo Woman'. During a recession, budget travel articles are sought. And if eco-tourism is the latest buzz word, consider a Galapagos story. Keep track of these pseudo popularity contests and write about their *finalists*.

I've learned a lot I could not have learned if I were not a writer.

William Trevor

Work full time or part time

In conjunction with my writing, I have simultaneously worked as a hotel concierge, travel agent, editor, on-site convention coordinator and correspondent for a travel trade magazine.

Because of these work experiences, I've been asked what's best – a part-time writing-related or non-writing-related job. The choice is a subjective one because positive motivations vary from one writer to the next. There are two schools of thought regarding the part-time job question.

One is that coupling travel writing with an additional writing-related job constantly keeps you in a writer's state of mind, as opposed to siphoning energy and directing it towards an unrelated area. On the opposition side are those who believe getting away from the creative demands of writing and into an unrelated field renews energy for the written word.

For me, the best combination is to mix my travel writing with a non-writing but travel industry-related job. This duo helps me grow as a travel expert and rejuvenates my writing spark. While the choice is up to you, some of these decisions are not always based on what works best creatively but on what is best financially.

Freelancer Beth D'Addono comes from a different perspective, accepting work as long as it's writing:

I've found a good match with one local firm – I write for them one or two days a week, primarily on legal, health and business topics, ghostwriting for their clients, writing trade articles, op-eds (opinion editorials), etc.

I have the benefit of going into an office a few times a week (access to resources, copy machine, etc. – I pay for copies but don't have to go to the Kinkos to do it), and also have the benefit of office camaraderie, ordering out lunch, etc.

This has worked well for me; I can count on a certain income and still pursue my own work, including travelling whenever I need to. It's a perfect arrangement, one that has been in place for five years.

You are independent

Beyond the travel, one of the profession's prime draws is the independence travel writing offers, particularly to the freelancer. As a freelancer, you'll most likely operate from a home office where the dress code can be warmups in winter, shorts and a tee-shirt in summer.

My commute is ten seconds down the hall to my office. My hours vary. I may work 10 am to 3 pm one day and 11 pm to 3 am the next. And on days devoted to research review I might choose to take my mounds of printed materials and highlighting pen, along with a lounge chair and sunglasses, to the beach where I work uninterrupted on the edge of the surf. My work day is not carved in stone.

What is certain, however, is that after years of this described structure (or lack of it), I would be unhappy in a traditional 9 am to 5 pm job.

The big motivation for me was the desire to be independent, to get up when you want, write what you want and work where you want.

Irving Wallace

Bountiful benefits

Fringe benefits surround you. An obvious perk of the job is worldwide travel which translates to very lucrative benefits. Over the past several years, I have experienced travel opportunities with a net worth of over US $50,000. And in addition to assorted trips, airfares, hotel stays and restaurant meals, my fringe benefits have included complimentary golf lessons/golf rounds, front row theatre tickets and signature spa treatments.

I've been chauffeured from the airport to an island's exclusive resort. But I've also ridden on a steamy, crowded South American bus with the locals, their dogs and chickens. Such is the life of a travel writer.

Financial realities

If you've chosen a career in travel writing because you believe it's extremely lucrative, you've selected the wrong profession. Many travel writers make only enough to pay for their journeys by selling their stories to newspapers and magazines. Then there are times that pay for an article equates to a nice profit. And at the opposite end of the spectrum is the beginner who writes for a byline but no pay.

In his *Writer's Market* article entitled 'A Writer's Guide to Money', Gary Provost warns would-be writers:

> *If you want to understand how writers make money you must first lose a lifetime of assumptions about work and money. Specifically, you must delete these three ideas from your mind: My pay is related to the number of hours I work (the hourly wage); my pay is related to the number of items I produce (piecemeal); my pay is related to the quality of my work (merit).*

Thus, the time-worn saying, 'A fair day's wages for a fair day's work', simply doesn't apply to writing for a living.

Your byline

Seeing your name in print may be the most fulfilling reason for writing travel articles – *your* byline alongside *your* words. For me, it's this reward that almost negates the financial realities of my chosen career.

Are *you* a travel writer?

Do you have what it takes? Do you love to travel? Do you even want to be a travel writer? Each time I get on a plane, walk onto the promenade of a cruise ship or step aboard a train to go to work, my answer's a resounding yes. But my answer is unimportant. This book is written to help *you* make that determination.

Words of writing wisdom

... from the beginning

Katharine Dyson has experience on both sides of the desk: as the editor of a travel trade magazine, *Jax Fax Travel Marketing*, and as a freelance writer for consumer and trade publications.

From the beginning, I could not decide whether to be a writer or an artist. So I did both, studying art and journalism in college and going on to publish regional guides in Connecticut. My children were young at the time, so I did all the writing, design and marketing from my home office. Later, when the position of editor of Jax Fax *became available, a job that required not only editorial skills but the ability to lay out the pages of the publication as well, I felt I could do it thanks to the experience I'd already had with my own magazines.*

The first few months on the job required a huge amount of work, not only to do the job but to learn what the travel industry was all about. For months I devoured every travel publication I could get my hands on. I read on the trains, on the plane, even in the morning while I blow-dryed my hair. Representing the magazine at several trade shows, I got to know industry people, interviewed them, listened to countless speeches and attended seminars. This was important. Before you write about travel, you really have to do your homework, know what you are writing about and know your readers.

For the past ten years, I have been working as a freelancer. If you want to make enough to pay your bills, work is the key word. Just as I did as an editor, I treat my profession as a full-time job. My friends don't always understand this, and call me to go out and play. And I do. Sometimes. That's the up-side of freelancing. But when I take time off to play golf or tennis, I know I will most likely need to make up the time lost either at night or on the weekend.

02 getting started

As a beginning freelancer your home office may be the kitchen table, the rocking chair in the upstairs bedroom or a windowless nook in the basement. Many a travel article has been written from less glamorous locales. Yet it is probably in your best interest to create the most pleasing work environment possible.

Ideally your workspace should be *yours*. My at-home office has evolved from a desk crowded into my bedroom to an extra room furnished as a traditional office, complete with a desk, phone, computer, printer, fax machine and Internet access.

On one side of my office is a bookcase lined with reference books and adorned with on-the-job souvenirs like hand-carved Fijian bookends. And above my desk are visual reminders of my travels – coloured photos of yours truly in Rome, or Hong Kong or wherever. You see, it is important to remind myself that on many of the days when I'm not working at my desk, I'm visiting the world.

Office setup

Whatever workspace you assign yourself, strive for the following: good lighting, a nearby window, an ergonomically safe and comfortable chair, pleasing temperature (avoid the warmest and coldest areas of the house) and a quiet atmosphere away from the household bustle. And, if possible, select an area that does not necessitate daily setup and tear down. This regular chore simply robs a journalist of precious writing time and may provide one more reason not to start. Your ultimate goal is to carve out an office area that says '*It's time to work*' once you sit down.

Thousands of people plan to be writers, but they never get around to it.

Judith Krantz

Computer's a must

Now add the essential tools of the travel writing trade. While many authors have penned a classic epic with pencil and paper and many more with a typewriter, a computer is essential to today's journalist. Yes, *essential*.

It seems most anti-computer journalists fear the learning curve. I understand. I confess to being the type of cook who resisted the microwave for years. 'Who needs to re-learn how to prepare food', I protested. However, the advice I impart from one traditionalist to another is: if you can type, you can use the computer. If you're intimidated, take a computer class. And if you choose to utilize your computer as a word processor alone, so be it. However, it is important to note a growing number of newspapers and magazines prefer that writers e-mail stories and some *only* work with freelancers who can telecommunicate their stories.

This 20th century invention has advanced the traditional writing process by light years. A computer allows you to write, edit, cut and paste before printing a single page of text. And even the simplest of computers can number pages, count words, check spelling, check grammar, act as a thesaurus, address envelopes, provide a choice of typefaces and track article submissions. One word of caution is to be aware of the fallibility of most computers' spell and grammar features. (Remember a computer can't distinguish between *their* and *there*.)

My dependence on the computer was underscored several years ago when my 10-year-old wrote a paper about her family life without electricity. Kathryn stated that under those circumstances her mother would not be a writer. I reminded her that in previous centuries one wrote by daylight or candlelight to which my daughter replied: 'Mom, you couldn't write because you wouldn't have a computer.' I realized she was correct.

Other essential equipment

In addition to a computer, essential office equipment in a travel writer's arsenal should include a printer that produces letter-quality documents, a dedicated telephone line fax machine, a telephone with an answering machine and the call-waiting feature and complete Internet access. Try to acquire dual-functioning items like a fax machine which also makes simple copies. And purchase brand name equipment to ensure quality and ease of repairs.

Other office enhancements include bookshelves for reference materials and cabinets for the mounds of brochures, press kits, maps and assorted files.

Recorder ins and outs

A portable, lightweight tape recorder with a telephone attachment is helpful for telephone and in-person interviews. Select one that is unobtrusive. The optimum recorded interview situation is obtained when the subject forgets he is being recorded. The following illustrates a typical interview scenario.

You've asked the interviewee if he minds the use of a recorder. (You must always do so.) Your subject has no objection. Under these circumstances, it is best to explain that the recorder is used only as a reference and place it in a non-threatening position. Then proceed to take notes throughout the interview. This orchestrated process puts the subject at ease and maximizes the possibility for the most natural and sharpest quotes.

A recorder can also be useful when on the road. Many travel writers carry this piece of equipment to chronicle all audio aspects of a visit, from a tour guide's verbal presentation to an on-site interview with a local innkeeper. This method captures every spoken fact but also requires many transcription hours.

In order to streamline the process, some travel writers use the recorder as a piece of personal dictation equipment. For example, during a lengthy city tour you, the travel writer, repeat only relevant facts divulged by the guide into the recorder. And don't neglect using this device to preserve eternally a destination's distinctive ambience, whether it's sheep bleating at daybreak in New Zealand or the verbal banter that punctuates Seattle's early-morning fish market.

The savvy travel writer also makes verbal note of personal observations during the exploration stage. Discreetly speaking into a compact recorder you might say: 'The lobby is slightly worn, yet projects a homey, comfortable feel. Velvet curtains frame the view of the meadow. The aroma from the nearby kitchen suggests a meat and potatoes lunch.' To a casual observer, it may appear you talk to yourself. Who cares! What I see is someone who wisely economizes his time.

A picture says a 1000 words

Bear in mind that note-taking and verbal reminders must be supplemented by photographs. Record facts. Make note of the atmosphere, the overall environment, whether or not the staff is friendly. But don't neglect to record every step of the trip on film.

Photography has often been called an additional form of note-taking. Snap photographs in lieu of jotting down every minute detail. One photo can replace a page of notes detailing a hotel room's colour scheme, its marble fireplace and the carved maple headboard. You get the picture.

You must of course have a camera in order to accomplish this pictorial assignment. A 35mm fully automatic camera with auto-focus, auto-flash and auto-film advance is a good selection for the amateur photographer, as it is for many of today's travel writing veterans. Digital is another option. Again, purchase a brand name because it is easier to get an internationally recognized camera like Nikon, Canon or Olympus repaired while on foreign soil.

Photography, including camera selection and camera equipment, will be discussed in greater detail in Chapter 12. However, there are several additional supplies that aid the writer/photographer. A photo journal should be kept listing by frame number and roll number (use a felt-tipped pen to designate the roll number on the metal film canister) each photograph taken, place and person (if applicable). This process takes time but is helpful when your 20 rolls of developed film return and it's been three weeks since your month-long tour of Korea.

In order to identify photography (prints and slides) as yours, a rubber stamp imprinted with your name, address and telephone number is helpful. Keep in mind the stamp must be small for use on 35mm slide mounts. And a small, portable light table and a loop (for magnification) are a must when working with slides.

Reference books

Helpful books for the travel writer go well beyond the customary dictionary, thesaurus and atlas. Additional reference items include quotation books, grammar books, style and usage books, how-to travel writing and photography books, the Bible, encyclopedias, guidebooks, foreign dictionaries, foreign cookbooks and pictorial coffee table books. (For lists of helpful resources, refer to the references section at the end of the book.)

Get organized

Once you've set up shop and acquired the trade's tools, it's time to organize. Set up files. If you are travelling to a certain destination or have a particular interest in a destination, make a file. As you come across articles, brochures and other information regarding the destination, place them in the file. Note that travel articles aren't exclusively about destinations. They can be travel related, addressing topics like combating jet lag or packing light. Start an in-the-future file for travel items that capture your interest.

File publications like newspaper travel sections, in-flight magazines, consumer magazines, travel trade magazines, regional city publications and other periodicals that are possibilities for submission. Perusal of these newspapers and magazines can give the travel writer endless ideas for potential travel pieces.

It is because of the plethora of support material you must collect that an orderly filing system is essential. As a travel writer who recently replaced five cardboard boxes with three attractive wicker floor files, I admit to being flawed somewhat in this area. However, the following tips may be employed to maintain optimum organization.

Colour code frequently used file folders by categories. For example, one colour can be reserved for hotel information and another for airline news. Or one colour can represent material collected from your visit to France (and broken into sub-categories like restaurants, museums, lodging, etc.) while another colour's folders are reserved for a different destination. Remember, there is no right or wrong system. The right system for you is your system, so personalize it to meet your needs.

Cross-reference files if necessary. Eliminate a miscellaneous file, which always becomes a magnet for assorted odds and ends. And annually review your files to purge them of unneeded materials.

When in the throw-away mode, ask yourself several questions. Is this material outdated? Can updated material easily be obtained? (It may be more difficult to get information from Bahrain than the Bahamas.) Is the information public relations fluff or is it relevant? If the information was used in an already published article, do I intend to rewrite or reslant the piece? Even if I have no intention of reusing the research, it is my policy to keep material supporting a published piece for six months in case questions arise from a reader.

A system for business cards is equally important. I file business cards by category, whether it's cards collected from the press trip to Aruba, acquired at a writing seminar or received while working on a Canadian destination piece. I then staple the business card onto an index (Rolodex) card. This system works for me. Remember, whatever system you employ, the key is to use it.

Develop an idea notebook

Many beginners fear they will run out of ideas for travel articles. Poppycock! Your specialty is the world and we live in a big world. However, it is smart to start a list of article possibilities. This practice reassures the novice and reminds the veteran of future story options.

'Where do you get the ideas?' you may ask. Everywhere. Other travel articles trigger your variation of the same idea. For instance, 'San Francisco's Ten Trendiest Boutiques' becomes 'London's Ten Most Distinctive Antique Stores'. Don't neglect your surroundings. Your everyday environs are loaded with ideas, whether it's your town's annual Christmas parade or your city's century-old opera house. Keep in mind what may be ho-hum to you can be exotic and exciting to an editor on the opposite side of the world. Once you begin this list, you will be amazed at its length.

Act like an expert

As a travel writer you're expected to be a professional – to present yourself professionally in person, on paper and by phone. You may be in your bathrobe when you answer your first business call of the day. However, it is important to sound as if you are all-business.

My standard telephone greeting, 'Hello, this is Cynthia Dial', is multi-purposed. I want to project a professional image and I want to remind my well-intended friends that I am working. I also established an edict early on for my family. During work hours, only I answer the telephone, eliminating the possibility of: 'Mom, it's for you.'

Because your initial introduction to an editor is almost always by correspondence, the first step toward a proficient look requires a small but crucial investment in the printing of letterhead, matching envelopes, matching mailing labels (if the budget allows) and, most importantly, business cards.

Business card scoop

While business cards vary from one travel writer to the next, professionalism is key. My business card is straightforward. The typeface is the same as my letterhead. And in addition to including the vital statistics, my job title is listed as writer/photographer. Titles can be wordsmith, scribe, photojournalist, writer/editor or simply travel writer.

I've seen business cards of travel writers listing professional affiliations, areas of specialization (family travel, adventure travel, etc.) or the inclusion of a small colour photograph of the writer on location. While these cards are memorable, I prefer to keep it simple.

Business cards should be distributed liberally – in person and with each piece of correspondence sent. Always carry your business cards. I keep three fully stocked card cases – for my purse, my briefcase and my camera bag. Business cards are particularly useful when travelling internationally, where otherwise closed doors are easily opened with the credibility created by this small but powerful 2″ × 3½″ piece of paper.

One travel writer I know makes a point of writing a note to everyone whose business card she collects. While this habit is time consuming, it carries networking to the next level and has paid dividends for this journalist time and again.

All about the letterhead

Give time and thought to your business card and letterhead. They represent you, often in your absence. Letterhead should be printed on white or off-white plain bond paper and imprinted with black or dark grey ink. Select an easily readable typeface. The letterhead should include your name, address, telephone number, fax number, e-mail address and website, if applicable.

A novice sometimes thinks his letterhead must be distinctive to get an editor's attention. Forget the fuchsia stationery or artwork of a harried travel writer with a camera on one shoulder and luggage on the other. This is not the time to be creative. It's the time to be professional. And trust me, an editor, as well as a business acquaintance, will respond to a professional look more favourably than one that shouts *beginner*.

Dress the part

Although most interactions (especially for the beginner) may be by snail mail or e-mail, face-to-face encounters are inevitable. Get over the notion that appropriate attire for a writer is a wrinkled shirt, jeans and dirty tennis shoes. While we may be considered an unconventional bunch, I know few writers who want to project a sloppy image and even fewer editors who are impressed by it.

I try to use common sense when selecting meeting attire. For example, I wore a business suit, hosiery and heels when I travelled to Texas for an interview with a Continental Airlines vice-president. Yet, I dressed in jeans and a denim shirt when I met with a California cowboy at his Malibu ranch. I later applauded my choice of outfits as I stood in the middle of a horse corral to get the action shots necessary for my travel article. The interview itself was conducted as we ate tuna sandwiches while sitting at his Formica kitchen table.

Had I dressed in a business suit and heels to interview my Malibu cowboy, I doubt he would have felt comfortable sharing the priceless nuggets we discussed over our casual lunch. And, conversely, the airline executive rightfully would have been insulted had I arrived in jeans. Your aim is not to be a mirror image of your contact, but your job does require you to relate – whether it's with a hotel general manager, a museum curator, a new editor or a potential agent.

Become editor savvy

Most editors are noted for their to-the-point, straightforward manner and all are overworked. Thus, certain skills are helpful when dealing with them. Incorporating the following tips into your standard writer/editor repertoire will help pave the way for a solid business relationship.

Your first contact with an editor should be by correspondence, as opposed to the telephone. And whether it's your first or fiftieth contact with an editor, take very little of his time. Get to the point (by written correspondence, e-mail or phone). When speaking by telephone, avoid chitchat but do follow the editor's lead. If he was getting married when you spoke six months ago and he's in a talkative mood, ask about his wife. Don't hound an editor and never argue. If he's not interested in an idea, he's not interested. Be honest. Always project a pleasant image (try speaking on the telephone with a smile on your face). And as you should in any personal dealing, maintain a sense of humour.

Writing is a business

'I am faithfully at my desk between 8 am and 9 am and usually work until 6 pm, before heading out for evening assignments a few times a week', says writer Beth D'Addono of her work routine. 'I'm a morning person, so if I'm on top of a deadline, I get up at the crack of dawn instead of staying up late at night to get it done – that works better for me.'

The most blessed thing about being an author is that you do it in private and in your own time.

Agatha Christie

'Travel writing or any writing for that matter requires commitment and discipline', says freelancer Katharine Dyson. 'Sure you can reward yourself with a vacation or a day off, but when you're working at home, resist the temptation to put another load in the washing machine or dig in the garden unless you have control of your projects and deadlines. It's all too easy to get sidetracked.'

Approach writing as if it were a business ... because it is a business. Set regular office hours. Budget your time and budget your energy. Remember, good writing is about organization. And while the writing lifestyle attracts an easy-going, unorthodox following, the life of a successful writer shouts for structure.

03 trip prep

In this chapter you will learn:
- all about formal and informal research
- steps to take before leaving home
- packing and health considerations.

Now that your workplace is set – files are in place, bookshelves are filled with reference materials and the computer, fax and Internet are ready to go – it's time for you to go. But before you get on the airplane to begin your on-location investigation, certain ground preparations are necessary.

The first step is research

To many, the word *research* is not a popular one. Perhaps this is because it is associated with our student days, spending hour upon laborious hour in a dark corner of the library. But to a travel writer research is essential, it's varied and it can be fun.

What is research? Travel research can be as formal as a day at the library or as informal as a conversation over cocktails about your neighbour's latest vacation. More than likely, your most valuable explorations will be lifted from a casual telephone conversation, from a discussion with your local travel agent or from a back issue of your community newspaper's travel section. Travel talk is everywhere.

The purpose of fact finding is multifaceted. Probes, both formal and informal, can help you decide where to go.

Informal research

The owner of ABC Travel may say India is this year's top vacation destination. Perhaps several well-travelled friends recently have mentioned a little known Mexican haven called San Miguel de Allende. Or let's say you overheard a conversation between two ski buffs about a pristine, yet undiscovered Montana resort. Each of these encounters can be influential, but don't neglect your library or librarian.

Formal research

When researching or writing about a subject in depth, your local research librarian should become one of your best friends. Invest in this important relationship by introducing yourself personally. Explain that you are a travel writer and will be drawing upon their expertise. Rather than spending a day at the library delving through stacks of materials to unearth obscure facts, call this expert. My librarian has assisted me on a variety of facts – from the name and height of Kuala Lumpur's skyscraper (the world's tallest) to the amount of pasta served annually in Italy.

The *Reader's Guide to Periodical Literature* (or its computerized equivalent) is located in the library's reference section. This publication lists when and where articles were printed within the last ten years by subject, enabling you to review what other writers like yourself have penned about India or San Miguel de Allende or any other destination. But using the *Reader's Guide* tells you much more. Is your subject popular? Has it been published ad nauseam or has it never been published? Has your target market recently published a similar article? This helpful information may confirm the proposed story's potential or suggest you seek another topic.

Other valuable library references are the *Times of London Index* and *New York Times Index*, giving the date, page and column for articles written on subjects in each of the respective newspapers. The *Christian Science Monitor* and the *Wall Street Journal* publish similar indexes.

Research is not a complicated science. Bear in mind that the obvious sources of information are often the best. Pursue those first. My first pass at researching a subject begins with a look at the *World Book Encyclopedia*, which was purchased when my university student daughters were beginning their elementary education. Yes, it's old but it has valuable and timeless information. This resource gives me a quick expansive overview of my intended subject.

My next stop may be a travel book. Guidebooks are full of facts and most include maps. While some may consider these books only valuable to the leisure traveller, this is not the time to reinvent the wheel. Why should I set the car odometer to measure the distance between Jerusalem and Tel Aviv when an Israel guidebook contains the information. Be aware that although these books come out annually, much of the material is outdated by as much as two years. So double-check time-sensitive facts.

The American Automobile Association and the British Automobile Association are possible sources for touring maps, an indispensable travel writing tool and an increasingly difficult one to obtain. And if you're planning a road trip, member services for these organizations can include custom-made trip kits for car travellers.

The Internet has changed the world of research. This relatively new tool makes fact exploration effortless, even for the most obscure destination. However, the infinite amount of information available through the Net is both a travel writer's dream and a potential nightmare. Resist the temptation to become an Internet research junkie, learn how to narrow your search and remember that not all research found in this medium is accurate and up to date.

Resourceful research

Other resources I traditionally employ are the public relations department or director of a local attraction, chambers of commerce, convention and visitor bureaus (CVBs) and tourism offices (see references section at the end of the book).

It makes CVB sense …

'A CVB should be a travel writer's first stop for information and referrals', says Charles Leong, senior executive with the Singapore Tourism Board. 'Any missing gaps could then be filled by other avenues of research like Web sites, travel industry contacts and people who visited the destination previously (and preferably recently).

'A CVB's primary role is destination marketing. Hence, it is an invaluable source of information on what to do, where to go, what to buy, what to see, where to stay, where to eat, etc. etc.'

I request a press (or media) kit from each of these resources already mentioned, who are usually eager to comply. A press kit can include an assortment of materials like brochures, booklets, press releases, a facts sheet, maps and photographs.

In-flight magazines and in-room hotel magazines (printed and distributed by major hotel chains) are also good sources of destination information. Say I'm flying KLM Airlines to Holland. In advance of my departure I'll request the national carrier's in-flight publication. Likewise, I always inquire if a hotel distributes an in-room magazine (like Radisson Hotel's *Voyageur* magazine); and if so, I ask if it can be mailed to my home to acquaint me with the city before my arrival.

Go native before you go

Several weeks before leaving home I frequent a major bookstore in my area known to carry international publications and purchase a local newspaper from the destination I will visit. (A comprehensive newsstand can serve the same purpose.) This exercise immerses me in the local scene. To further this sense of place, my choices for casual reading include books with the city or country as a backdrop, like James Michener's *Mexico*.

Language books, even a basic language course for lengthier stays, help a travel writer blend into the destination. I personally recommend *Worldwide Multilingual Phrase Book: Survival Skills for over 40 Languages*. But for those who profess to be linguistically challenged, my advice is to learn the foreign language basics like *hello*, *goodbye*, *please*, *thank you*, *how much*, numbers 1 to 10 and *where's the bathroom* (for the more ambitious).

Plot your trip path

Nuts-and-bolts research tells you how to travel, which airline flies to your selected destination, where to stay, where and what to eat, what to do (top sites), what time of year is best, native customs, local industries and best buys. Pre-trip inquiries are essential and are time saving because the travel writer becomes intimately familiar with the destination before ever setting foot on its soil. This kind of scrutiny helps the visitor/journalist plot his trip path.

I never resent or attempt to shortcut this process because I recall my near-wasted visit to Brussels. As a university student, I made my first trip abroad upon graduation. Because my school years were glutted with research, I refused to research what I considered a vacation. Thus, my first visit to Europe was a combination of chance visits to historic sites and missed opportunities.

It was due to my lack of knowledge of Belgium's capital that I aimlessly wandered through the city's streets before stumbling upon Brussels' showpiece, its main square called Grand' Place, which literally overflows with ornate 17th-century buildings. Whenever I tend to resent pre-trip preparation, I simply *remember Brussels*, a sure cure for a momentary lapse in my desire to research adequately.

Develop a writing plan

After attending a South American seminar several years ago, I became so enthralled with Ecuador and the Galapagos Islands it warranted a visit. Even before renewing my passport, my agenda was roughly set as a result of a compilation of information culled from seminar speakers, brochures, guidebooks and recent Ecuadorian visitors. This advance preparation paved my way to a maximized visit. How did my Ecuadorian trip shape up? I chose to concentrate on three specialized areas of interest: the Galapagos, Otavalo Market and Riobamba train ride.

Located 600 miles off the coast of Ecuador, the Galapagos Islands were selected for what I considered obvious reasons. They are noted for their one-of-a-kind distinctive animals and plants. Biologist Charles Darwin introduced these islands to the world during his studies of their animal and plant life when he developed his theory of evolution. This being said, a Galapagos cruise was a must.

Noted as one of South America's premier markets, Otavalo is famous for this event. Dating back to pre-Inca times Saturday's gathering really features two markets. The local market is for buying and bartering animals, food and other essentials. And the more tourist-driven bazaar overflows with colourful crafts and clothing, including the famed Panama hat.

One of the more picturesque aspects of Otavalo is the traditional way of dress. The men are noticeable because of their long single pigtail, calf-length white pants and dark felt hats. The women are equally striking with intricately embroidered blouses, long black skirts and head cloths, whose colour and style denotes marital status. But my most memorable photographs featured young Otavaleno children pulling the family goat, pig or other farm animal by a single rope to the local market for trade.

While it no longer operates between the two cities, the Riobamba train experience between Cuenca and Quito promised adventure. The opportunity to climb an outside ladder (as the train chugged down the tracks) in order to sit atop the car was irresistible. The trick was to remain alert because of the necessity to lie down when approaching low hanging electrical lines and undersized tunnels.

Once I determine my areas of concentration, I develop a writing plan. Possible Ecuadorian stories included the Galapagos, the Otavalo animal barter market, the Otavalo crafts market, history of the Panama hat (developed in Ecuador opposed to Panama) and shopping in Ecuador. The inclusion of Cuenca in my itinerary represented additional article options like the Riobamba train experience, the distinctive dress of the Cuenca resident versus the Otavaleno native, the colonial river city of Cuenca (Ecuador's third largest town) and the nearby fortress of Ingapirca (the country's best-preserved, pre-colonial ruin).

Let me walk you through my thought process. After anticipating three articles each from the Galapagos, Otavalo and the Cuenca region and two general Ecuadorian pieces (shopping and Panama hat), it's time to determine the logistics. Is it possible to fit my needs into a 14-day time frame, accommodating a Saturday (the only day for the animal market) visit to Otavalo, the Riobamba train (requiring advance reservations) and a Friday-departure cruise? We'll put it on paper and see:

Day 1 (Thursday)	Arrival Quito
Day 2–3 (Friday/Saturday)	Depart for Otavalo. Otavalo animal/craft market
Day 4–5 (Sunday/Monday)	Return and stay in Quito
Day 6–8 (Tuesday–Thursday)	Cuenca. Riobamba train to Quito
Day 9–13 (Friday–Tuesday)	5-day Galapagos cruise
Day 14 (Wednesday)	Return to Quito for departure

Mission accomplished. As you might imagine, Ecuador's offerings are plentiful. How did I narrow my inclusions to these three regions in a country covering over 100,000 square miles? Once again, research.

Is it doable?

In-depth research unearths a surplus of story ideas. However, not every potential idea is doable. Before visiting Portugal and during my pre-trip scrutiny of the regions on which I planned to concentrate, local pastry shops were repeatedly mentioned. Many villages featured their own specialty like Caldas Da Rainha's dessert delight called *cavacas*, a kind of meringue piled layers high with dripping sugar.

Understandably, I envisioned visiting a variety of these gastronomic havens, sitting at a corner table, sipping coffee and sampling the sugar-laden specialty as I visited with the mom or pop baker. Once in the country, however, I realized this delicious piece was not to be because the pastry shops were as busy as a New York City delicatessen at lunchtime. The Portuguese bakers in these small towns spoke no English. And I spoke no Portuguese. It quickly became apparent that chasing this particular story idea would be a tremendous investment in both time and calories.

Pre-trip query

Once I've narrowed my focus to likely story possibilities, it's time to concentrate on pre-trip queries and contact editors about advance assignments. The query, which will be fully addressed in Chapter 08, is a one-page letter designed to entice an editor to give you an assignment.

Basically, a pre-trip query letter follows the same format as a post-trip query:

1 an arresting lead
2 why you should write the piece
3 a request for the assignment.

However, several additional items must be included when your query involves an upcoming trip. These inclusions are your departure and return dates and when the editor will receive the completed article. Send your pre-trip query in time to receive a reply before departure – anywhere from two to six months.

Letters of assignment

The primary purpose of pre-trip queries is to get letters of assignment. These coveted letters result in getting financial assistance in your airfare, hotel accommodation, ground transportation, even for excursions. They also give you on-location credibility, establish you as a proven professional and open doors closed to the mere novice.

Additional credibility can be established with copies of recent articles, a copy of the publication printing your article and a current bio. And don't forget the business cards – liberally distribute them to contacts as well as colleagues.

Letters of assignment make your job easier. If you know what you can sell before the trip, you can custom design your travels. This knowledge enables you to target your exact needs upon arrival and minimize wasted on-the-road hours.

Set up interviews

While knowing assignments in advance dictates which interviews should be pre-arranged, it is equally important to create an interview when no articles have been pre-assigned. Let's say you plan to write about the King Tutankhamen exhibit at Cairo's Egyptian Museum. You should contact the museum curator. And if you plan to focus on the ever-increasing role of the concierge while in London, you might want to arrange an interview with the Ritz Hotel's Michael de Cozar, a revered industry professional.

Regardless of your slant, try to arrange interviews and appointments well in advance. Keep in mind that negotiating some interviews may take persistence. In some countries and with certain dignitaries, a letter of introduction could be required; and in these cases consulates, embassies and national tourist organizations may be of assistance. But whatever channel must be pursued, the difference between getting or not getting a key interview can be as simple as starting the process early on.

Put on your travel agent hat

Once you've tackled the library research, gone on-line for additional information, established a rough itinerary, sent pre-trip queries and received a handful of letters of assignment, you're ready to chart your final course and plan the trip. Should you use a travel agent? Probably not, unless the relationship is long standing and he understands your needs.

Your travel needs are atypical. You're not the traditional leisure traveller. Thus, it is probably easier to make your own arrangements, especially if you're seeking financial assistance from hotels, airlines or government tourist boards. Plus, this hands-on planning process will give you additional familiarity with the area.

A travel writer's needs are both precise and complex. When setting up your itinerary, include what's old and what's new. See the common and the uncommon. Make a plan that allows you to be a tourist and *become* an insider. And even if you don't intend to write about it, visit the area's most famous site. In other words, don't overlook the Louvre while in Paris.

Is the time right?

Consider timing. Does your visit coincide with a national holiday? If so, will the stores, museums, etc. be closed? Or maybe it represents one-of-a-kind parades and festivities. Does everything close midday for siesta (as in Mexico)? Is the Sabbath celebrated on Saturday, as it is in Israel, shutting down everything from Friday afternoon to late Saturday night?

What about off-season travel? Summer in Phoenix is considered comfortable if the temperature registers less than 100° Fahrenheit. The Caribbean's off season and hurricane season overlap. Winter in London represents the best buy but it is usually cold and dreary at that time. This combination spells discomfort, as well as uninspired photography. Conversely, off-season travel can represent no queues, few tourists and great value. If money is an issue, consider travelling during shoulder season – the weeks between off season and high season – when the price is reasonable and the risks minimal.

Now let's pack

This assignment is a difficult one because you should pack light and pack smart. With the inclusion of camera and recording equipment and perhaps a laptop (which I never carry due to my minimum-weight rule), your luggage is already weighty before you open the closet. Thus, clothing selections must be thought out carefully.

Before packing, I analyze my itinerary. Are there formal events? Do I need business attire? Is there hiking or snorkelling or any activity that requires special clothing? I pack for these special situations and then add innumerable casual pieces for my downtime, sightseeing and comfort.

My motto is: keep it basic. My core travel wardrobe is black, including shoes. Black is universally considered a smart and sophisticated colour choice and can be worn repeatedly before it requires dry cleaning. But beyond the basic blacks I pack as monochromatically as possible, mixing and matching everything. To add colour, I include scarves, belts and jewellery. Once on site, I can buy a piece of fun jewellery or a hand-painted scarf and blend with the local style of dress.

From experience and regardless of weather predictions, I've

learned to include long silk underwear, gloves, an umbrella, tennis shoes, a hat, a sweatshirt (comes in handy on long, cold airplane flights) and an extra pair of comfortable shoes. Three additional lifesavers have been a Swiss Army knife (for plucking eyebrows, opening wine or cutting thread), bubble bath and a rhinestone belt (to transform an outfit instantly to formal attire). *Note*: Since September 11 a Swiss Army knife must be packed in luggage that is checked into the aeroplane's hold.

I only use a suitcase on wheels and I limit baggage to one piece to be checked and one carry-on for camera equipment. (Avoid expensive and matched sets of luggage that draw attention.) Long ago I learned to economize space: to roll clothing (eliminating hangers), stuff socks into shoes, cover easily wrinkled items with plastic and use sample-size toiletries.

Included at the bottom of my luggage is a nylon bag to carry additional items if a shopping spree or the collection of numerous press kits is unavoidable. Many veteran travel writers also carry 12″ × 15″ mailing envelopes to fill with collected materials to send home throughout the trip.

Get ready, get set, go

I don't get jet lag. I simply refuse to. I don't have the time. But I don't attribute this fact to good genes or good luck. Rather, I see it as the result of common sense.

Once on board, I follow several guidelines. I avoid caffeine (in coffee, tea and soft drinks), heavy protein and rich foods; limit myself to one glass of wine and drink one quart of water for every four hours in the air. I set my watch to the time of my destination and begin thinking within the bounds of that time frame. If at 4 pm I board a plane in Los Angeles bound for Zurich, I set my watch to the Swiss time (1 am) and behave accordingly. So, after a light meal and a glass of wine, I'm ready to sleep.

And upon arrival, I immediately adapt to the local time. For daytime arrivals, I unpack, take a shower and go for a walk. Exposure to light is key to minimizing jet lag. If I lie down, it's for no more than 1½ hours. I plan an undemanding first day and I go to bed no earlier than 8 pm. And at the hint of a cold or sore throat, I take the maximum dosage of zinc lozenges.

Get ready, get set, get healthy – now go

Good health is a must for the optimum travel writing experience, because travel alone is physically depleting. Now add a heavy camera bag, luggage loaded with press packets and the demands to climb Sydney's Bridge or to hike into the Haleakala Crater because you're writing about them.

Get both your required and suggested immunizations. (Consult a travel clinic.) Prepare for your travels by jogging or walking each day. Don't neglect vitamins, especially Vitamin C and think healthy. Positive thinking goes a long way to keeping you healthy.

Don't forget to ...

- Get necessary immunization shots (with documented proof).
- Have valid passport.
- Obtain necessary visas or tourist cards.
- Get international driver's permit, if necessary.
- Xerox important documents (passport, visas, tourist cards, driver's licence or photo identification, credit cards, medical insurance) and keep separately from actual documents.
- Check and double-check electronic equipment like camera, flash, laptop computer, recording device. (Run a roll through the camera in advance.)
- Pack your camera with your carry-on luggage. (Never check it in with the cargo luggage.)
- Bring extra batteries and plenty of film – both can be very expensive in tourist destinations. (**Definition of plenty**: determine the maximum amount of film you need; then multiply by two.)
- Carry film in clear plastic bag for hand-check through airport security (eliminating x-ray exposure).
- Remember airline ticket, hotel and surface transportation vouchers.
- Bring written confirmation or, if not available, confirmation numbers for car, hotel, excursion reservations.
- Carry enough money in local currency to cover two days' expenses. (*Note*: Exchange money before returning from some countries like Western Samoa, whose currency is not recognized outside the country.)

- Include an extra pair of glasses or contact lenses (or the prescription).
- Bring prescriptive medicines, along with written prescriptions.
- Have over-the-counter cures for colds, flu and upset stomachs.

04

on location

In this chapter you will learn:
- how to dress while on the road
- the importance of observing a locale's inner working
- travel writers' travel tips.

You're an actor whose job is to absorb your surroundings, get into the role, become the part. One of the best ways to accomplish the task is through dress. What does this advice mean? Don't stand out as a foreigner. Blend in.

This may translate as donning a robe and head covering before entering a Malaysian religious shrine or leaving the shorts, halter top and other flesh-baring attire at home when you're on a Middle Eastern visit.

It is my Holland experience that comically underscores the cultural differences in dress. Visiting as a participant of a golf press trip, I was apprised of the expected attire – long (not short) pants, collared shirt and golf shoes (no tennis shoes). As a beginner, I was careful to follow the rules, not wishing to draw unwanted attention to myself. Thus, I carefully dressed for the outing at our first golf venue, a public course near Amsterdam.

As we approached the 9th hole I noticed spectators on the opposite side of a water hazard, standing hands on hips. Without my glasses it wasn't until I reached the green that I realized they had no clothes on. The course was next to a nudist camp and apparently two of its participants were golf enthusiasts as well. And I was concerned about wearing a collared shirt!

Put away the jeans for a *babushka*

As a frequent traveller I strive to dismiss the notion of the ugly American and steer clear of the typical jeans and tennis shoes uniform. I may wear bright, colourful clothing in a Mexican resort on one trip and a dark, solid *babushka* in Jerusalem on my next. And I never wear clothing that is considered offensive. In Egypt this dress edict meant slacks or an ankle-length skirt and a long-sleeved shirt. Locals notice the difference and appreciate the consideration because it shows you've observed how they dress and that you respect them. And from my observations, I've noticed that dressing in a familiar way makes people more eager to welcome a visitor and adds a certain degree of protection.

My traditional travel ensemble includes a long, black all-weather coat. In many countries, this outer garment serves a function beyond the obvious cold and rainy weather protector – I look like a local. This fact was underscored during a trip to

Lisbon with my husband, a tall, Swedish-looking blonde. While I easily recognized Kent in a crowd, he frequently lost me because as a small, dark-haired woman in a black coat, I merged into the sea of similarly attired Portuguese. My nondescript attire also makes me more approachable – I become less of a stranger.

Look like a local but be a tourist

Everyone tackles a new city differently – there is no right or wrong. This is my approach. As soon as I check into my hotel, I call and reconfirm interviews or set interviews I didn't arrange before leaving home.

Before setting out on my own I take a city tour to get my bearings, understand the city layout, see important landmarks and help determine to which of those sites I will return. I tour the city with a map, circling areas of interest in pen.

Because I try to stay in the city centre, it's usually an easy walk from my hotel to the oldest part of town – the area that best defines a locale. Walking is the best way to take the pulse of a city. If it's a metropolis, I use public transportation like a light rail system, bus, tram or metro (rarely a taxi). If I'm in London I take the tube at rush hour. And when in Bangkok I use the local water taxi along the Chao Phraya River, just as the orange-robed Buddhist monks do. My goal is to experience the destination as its residents do.

While I always have my notebook and camera, I do so incognito. I make note of details during my exploration and capture the locale on film, but I operate somewhat undercover. A stop at a café or a rest on a park bench doubles as an opportunity to soak up the local atmosphere and carefully pen my observations.

Make yourself at home

When at home I begin each morning with a power walk. And while on the road I do so as well. 'Can you afford the time?' you might ask. The daily ritual actually saves me time. Seeing a city in the wee morning hours is like seeing someone without makeup on. You see the natural beauty, blemishes and all. It's my favourite and most productive time of day to investigate.

During my early-morning exploration, I've witnessed Hawaiian tree trimmers swinging from tree to tree, Tarzan style, trimming errant palm fronds; Mexican hawkers walking their decorated *burros* to the Tijuana city centre for a day of photo opportunities with tourists; a clown-costumed juggler riding his bicycle to work at New Orleans' Jackson Square.

I've culled local tidbits from a pre-dawn trash collector, a vendor at the food market and a patron of a coffee house. What can these am revelations tell the travel journalist? How the destination wakes up. Whether its residents are hurried and rushed or laid back and relaxed.

Many a story can result from simply doing on the road what you do at home. I have attended mass at the Vatican, a traditional Hawaiian service with grass-skirted attendants and a Mexican church service alongside cats and dogs. One of my most memorable souvenirs, and a consequent story idea, remains a high-styled haircut experienced on the Caribbean island of St Barts. And don't forget the massage. I've had more types of massage than I have stamps in my passport – and each has been uniquely different.

Pursue your interests. If you've coached an American youth soccer team, go to a game of European football. An accomplished seamstress might want to visit fabric shops or designer clothing factories. And an avid stamp collector should stop at the local post office.

Shop at the corner grocery, explore the food stalls and the farmers' market, have a pint at the pub, visit a haute couture boutique, explore the local department store, visit an auction house, browse through an antique shop. This is one of the world's few jobs where shopping is mandatory, not frivolous.

Make museums and galleries, as well as wine bars and family-owned cafés, your haunts. Rub elbows with the locals, talk to the natives, become intimate with the area. Develop a sense of place.

Watch the city tick

Observe a city's inner workings. Tour a Cuban cigar factory. Witness a trial at London's Central Criminal Court (better known as the Old Bailey) or, if allowed, attend a session of the US House of Representatives in Washington DC's Capitol building.

Get behind the scenes. Visit the back lot of a movie studio. See the inner workings of a major sport's facility like Yankee Stadium. Arrange a backstage tour of a theatre. Tour a museum with a guide or docent to get in-depth background information.

Interact with locals

How do you open a conversation with strangers? Start with a smile. Be pleasant and non-aggressive. Pay a compliment to the country, the town, the café, the cuisine, whatever you sincerely like. Follow up with a request for information or advice. Avoid a discussion on politics and religion (listen to the locals and take their lead). Once a rapport is established, it's time to introduce yourself as a travel writer and ask if they would mind answering a few questions.

In addition to obvious questions, the following might be helpful. Is there folk lore known only to locals? What shouldn't be missed that few tourists know about? Is there a favourite, little-known museum? What is the most popular leisure activity? What do residents do on Sundays?

Or ask what might be considered a silly but legitimate question. With automobiles stacked two and three deep on the streets of Rome, I once asked a resident how the inside car gets out. I was told that the small cars are physically lifted and moved until the blocked vehicle can leave.

This type of informal interview has resulted in a collection of worldwide memories. After a morning tour of the tiny Greek island of Mykonos, my husband and I asked George, our taxi driver/tour guide, to stop for lunch and he invited us to his modest home to eat.

I treasure our meal of feta cheese, hummus and salad eaten on the white stucco picnic-like table under the warm Mediterranean sun. Our meal mates were George, his Greek-speaking wife, black-attired mother-in-law (still mourning her husband's death after 15 years) and his young son.

In addition to enjoying our newly found friends, I made mental note of everything. I noticed the picture of President Kennedy prominently displayed in the living quarters, the antique silver cross in the family chapel and George's goats wandering onto the nearby airport runway. (The airport calls George to remove his farm animals when a plane's approaching, we were told.)

What I observed was as important as what was said.

I've spent the evening in a Glasgow home entertained by a kilt-clad bagpiper and visited the apartment of my Egyptian tour guide, Noha, where I perused the wedding pictures of her and her new husband.

Relax as the locals

Sip a cappuccino in Rome, a Guinness in Dublin or ouzo, if you dare, in Athens. Bars and cafés are informal centres of information. Frequent them.

This advice doesn't mean to hang out at the Hilton or Marriott's coffee shop or the sleek Western-style bar that caters to visiting business executives. Rather go to a taverna or the corner bistro where people collect and talk about the grandchildren, the weather, the neighbourhood or politics. Even the smallest village has a gathering place, whether it's a store, a church or a diner.

Be a sleuth

Sherlock Holmes should have nothing on the curious travel writer. Every detail is a clue to the essence of a place. Street names tell volumes. Names like Bienville Avenue and Dauphine Street reflect the ambiance of New Orleans' French Quarter; whereas New York City's Avenue of the Americas and Mexico City's Paseo de la Reforma similarly create a telling impression.

The visual scene tells volumes about its people. Where do locals congregate? Are women huddled in one area and men another? Do all ages intermingle? How do children react to strangers? Do all ages, genders and economic groups appear in public areas? How do residents dress? Do they walk, ride bicycles – how do they get around? What is the street scene? (Are there street performers? Are homeless visible on the streets?) Is your presence as a stranger noticeable?

Eavesdrop and make mental notes. Develop a feel for society by listening to how people relate. Are the women assertive or subservient to men? Are children lively and animated or are they quiet and subdued? Are patrons polite to waiters or abrupt and demanding?

One anecdote plucked from this form of research was during a performance of the Glory of Easter at Southern California's famed

Crystal Cathedral. Sitting next to a young family, I overheard a little girl whisper loudly to her mother: 'I don't get it. This isn't about Easter. It hasn't said one thing about how the Easter Bunny was born.'

Explore inquisitively. Question everything. What kind of money is spent? Are there native handicrafts? What is the area's most noted site? How are meals observed? Is the evening meal long and leisurely? Or is the main meal served midday? Is the dinner hour at 10 pm or later? What are store hours? Are they open evenings? Do they close for several hours around midday? If so, do they siesta? Is there a lively night life? What entertainment options are available? Opera, live theatre, ballet, sporting events? What are the most popular leisure activities? *Jai alai*, bullfighting, football, surfing, sunbathing?

Notice posters, flyers, local newspapers, radio and television programmes. I remember once arriving in Ecuador. The political posters plastered around Quito's city centre told me it was election time. Devour daily newspapers. A local publication has many times alerted me to an upcoming festival or celebration. If that's the case, join in the fun. There's no better time to get to know people and receive a warm welcome than during a celebratory mood.

Micro versus macro

What is the story? Few editors have interest in a general destination article on London or Paris or Rome. But these same editors might be intrigued by a broad piece about Stratford-upon-Avon, Auvers-sur-Oise or the isle of Capri. Why would these smaller, lesser known sites in these respective countries be of greater interest than their celebrated capitals? The answer is simple. The less important the city, the larger the focus.

The converse is also true. The more important the city, the smaller the focus. This rule of thumb explains why a saleable London piece covers a Jack the Ripper tour, a Paris trip results in a story about the city's Chinatown found in its 13th arrondissement and a visit to Rome produces an article on the Vatican's colourful Swiss Guards.

Look for the extraordinary/ don't overlook the ordinary

The extraordinary story finds you; and when it does, you know it. As one of the first handful to make the Sydney Harbour Bridge climb, the piece shouted to be written. But the same trip also generated a story by a fellow traveller on a relatively ordinary topic – airline food.

Prompted by a personal tour of Qantas' catering kitchens in Sydney and an on-board sampling during the 18-hour Los Angeles/Sydney flight, the writer developed a food and drink piece. In the published newspaper article she incorporated in-flight eating tips to combat jet lag, a Qantas' in-flight food update and recipes of two of the international airline's light 'fly-save' main course salads. The moral of this story is not automatically to ignore and pigeonhole a subject as too common.

See the sights day and night

When viewing legendary landmarks, do so under an assortment of situations, from a variety of perspectives and at different times of day. See the Eiffel Tower during the day with the other tourists as you board one of its several elevators to the top. Return after dark to view and photograph the French icon. And, if your pocketbook allows, enjoy a meal within the structure's elite Jules Verne restaurant.

My photographs of the awe-inspiring Grand Canyon were taken at dawn, at dusk and most hours in between. The pictures display a unique spectrum of colours and a variety of contrasting moods (romantic, rugged, spiritual, challenging). But all say something distinctive about the 1-mile deep, 18-mile wide phenomenon.

Stop and smell the roses

Resist the temptation to stay on the travel writer treadmill. Get off and relax. Don't feel guilty – it's all research. Wander through a zoo. Sit on a wooden bench in the town square or stroll through a garden.

Between an exploration of Rome's Colosseum and a visit to the Vatican, my husband and I enjoyed a makeshift picnic with a fresh loaf of bread, cheese, and a bottle of Chianti in the Villa Borghese park.

Similarly a casual walk through London's Hyde Park on a clear, crisp Sunday afternoon was both a relaxing stroll and an entertaining respite from the typical bustle of the European capital. The afternoon was a combination of observing speakers, perched on individual ramshackle boxes, addressing controversial topics and young mothers pushing their babies about in prams.

Tour guide dilemma

A well-versed tour guide is worth the investment. Tour guides can save time; and when you're in a foreign destination thousands of miles from home for a limited period, your time can translate into big money. You can tour with a group or privately. If you select the group option, don't be embarrassed to stand near the front, take notes, snap photos, tape record if you desire and ask questions. And if you hire a private guide, tailor the tour to your needs. Note that it's wise to double-check facts shared by tour guides as some may tend to embellish.

After spending two weeks in the Republic of Ireland, another journalist and I opted to travel on our own to Northern Ireland during a ceasefire. Our time was limited to a day trip by train, binding us to a set schedule.

Upon arrival in Belfast we went to the city centre and hired a private driver/guide to tour the Protestant and Catholic areas. We asked the guide to concentrate on the troubled areas, because that's where the story was. The visual results included photographs of the Sinn Fein headquarters with a two-storey colour mural of activist Bobby Sands and an equally sensational visual of an oversized mural depicting a masked gunman with the verbiage, 'We will never accept a United Ireland. Uster says no.' Taken with a telephoto lens from the back seat of the vehicle, these dramatic photos more than compensated for the cost of the private tour.

Come rain or come shine

Coordinate outdoor explorations with the weather. If it's raining in the morning, postpone the hike or walking city tour and visit a museum or shopping area instead. Don't let weather alter your plans for a city. It could be a significant piece of the story puzzle.

Rain may be a way of life as it is in Seattle, where it's standard for a hotel concierge to distribute umbrellas and for bareheaded locals to walk in a steady mist as if the sun were shining. But certain locales can be altered by weather. A light powdering of snow, for example, has been known to paralyze cities like Washington DC or Dallas, Texas.

Consider inclement weather as research. How do locals react to the weather? Does the city slow to a crawl or does it bustle as usual? Do the people hibernate indoors or go about their normal business? Does talk of weather conditions dominate the news and casual conversations or is it ho-hum chitchat?

Local transportation

See a locale like a local. If it's a walking town like San Francisco, put on the comfortable shoes and head up and down the city's steep hills or jump on one of the California city's historic cable cars. Get a different perspective of Seattle from the water. Experience a mode of transportation used daily by commuters and ride the ferry boat to one of the area's outer islands. Or hop in a pedicab for a brisk ride through busy city streets on the Malaysian island of Penang.

And don't neglect exotic means of transportation. I've ridden a dog sled in Alaska, seen the pyramids by camel in Egypt and climbed aboard an elephant in Thailand. One of my more exciting transportation adventures was a city tour of Melbourne on the back of a Harley Davidson motorcycle.

Get lost!

Study a map. Get a general idea of the city layout, noting areas deemed unsafe. Then put the map in your backpack and take off. Or as an older brother says to a younger sibling: 'Get lost!'

Armed with a notebook, a camera and plenty of film, become the Ponce de Leon of travel writers and explore. Investigate back alleys, out-of-the-way haunts, hidden parks, low-profile neighbourhoods. These unknown routes become welcoming paths to the inquisitive travel writer.

Quiz your concierge

As soon as you arrive, introduce yourself to the concierge as a travel writer. Don't hesitate and miss a once-a-week event or a little-known annual celebration. I speak from experience. I continue to regret missing my opportunity to tour Buckingham Palace because my London arrival was the last day the royal family's residence was open to the public for the year. Unfortunately, I visited the concierge the following day.

Special arrangements and invitations for out-of-the-ordinary offerings are perks a concierge may eagerly extend to a working travel journalist. Thus, it's prudent to let this hotel ambassador know about you and your line of work. You may reap some benefits from this introduction. This is not advice to make demands, simply to make an acquaintance.

To journal or not to journal?

Remember, time muddles memory. So whether you call it a diary, travel log, notebook or journal, its contents are your record of first impressions. Don't forget that first impressions occur only once. These written notes, scribbled along the way, are invaluable in evoking atmosphere.

Before the image of an experience has a chance to fade, I notate the ruby red mush of grapes from the first pressing in Australia's Hunter Valley; reeds brushing the sides of a Nile cruising vessel; a Native American Indian in headdress drinking from a red and white Coca-Cola can. Someday these noted fragments of time will help me call to mind a scene and reproduce it accurately.

The travel journal is also replete with general observations, a tour guide's verbal input, simple quotes from locals, hard facts collected from historic plaques or road signs. Basic notations can serve the journalist in additional ways: for listing prices of handicrafts, a ferry schedule, the tour guide's name and address, museum hours, etc.

You may never forget holding a koala in Australia. But can you instantly recall how surprised you were that the grey marsupial was not soft and cuddly but coarse like a steel-wool cleansing pad? Reading my journal jogged this memory. My notations also reminded me that the furry creature was approximately 2½ feet in height and had white fur (not grey as my faulty long-term memory recalled) on its belly.

Note that even if there is little interest in writing a subsequent travel article, it's prudent to journal. The obvious reason is the journal's function to serve as an instant on-location recollection. But beyond this practical purpose is an additional reason. Say the trip doesn't generate the creation of a single travel article. Your journal then becomes a diary – a treasured memento.

Work is around the clock

Being a travel writer on location is like being a doctor on call. You're never off duty. But while travel research may include digging through volumes of documents in the dusty back room of a specialized library, it also entails dining in a city's newest five-star eatery and calling a presidential suite home for a couple of days.

What about writing on the road? There are two schools of thought. I know travel writers who carry laptops and write daily while on the road. Then there are those like myself who soak up the environment, let it marinate and regurgitate the experience on paper upon my return home. Hemingway said: 'Never write about a place until you're away from it, because it gives you perspective.'

First-time fears

Paralyzed is how many beginners feel on a first-time trip. What to do first? What to do next? What if no one will talk to me? Is the story doable? Can I sell it? Am I legitimate? The on-site answer to these fears is to concentrate on the basics: observations, notations, interviews and photography.

As a travel writer who has asked myself each of these self-doubting questions, this is my advice. Query yourself. Why am I travelling here (i.e. relaxation, activities, culture, cuisine)? What kind of readers would travel here? What would these readers want to know about the destination? What information do I need to be able to answer their questions?

Find the fun

If you're travelling halfway around the world to write about a distant place, it should be fun. And if it's not fun, stay home and write about something you already know about – something around the corner. Many prolific and successful travel writers do just that.

If, however, you're intrigued by the unfamiliar and the unknown and are energized by anything foreign, pull out the passport. Travel to exotic destinations to stay in a luxury hotel one night and a thatched hut the next. Experience the one of a kind. Get on the road and get paid for it. But have *fun*.

Don't forget to:

- visit bookstores
- devour local newspapers
- collect pamphlets, maps, menus, brochures, booklets (any literature of perceived or even unperceived value)
- buy postcards to recall unusual name spellings and visual details of important sites
- keep business cards of all contacts for contact information and to write thank you notes.

Words of writing wisdom

... life on the road

Connecticut-based Katharine Dyson has been a freelance travel writer for the past 20 years.

Travel writing can, by its nature, be tough on personal relationships. You travel, you come home, you write, you work nights and weekends and you travel. And so on. I happen to be lucky. I'm married to a man who understands what I do is a job. He knows when I am away, I am not on vacation. He knows because on a few occasions he has been invited along. But he knows although it sounds exotic and exciting, it is also hard work.

He encourages me to do what I have to do. He takes me to the airport, picks me up and reads through manuscripts giving me valuable input. If you share your life with someone else, having a good understanding with that person is vital. He or she has to be able to accept that in order to write about travel means being away often for days, even weeks. It goes with the territory.

But no matter how much I do not want to climb onto one more plane or waste any more hours on hard seats in an air terminal, once I reach my destination, I become energized. I love what I'm doing, the people I'm meeting, the sights and discoveries.

Then I come home, unwind and nail myself to my computer, some days so focused I forget to walk down the driveway and pick up the mail. Why do I do it? Because I like it. A lot.

05

the newspaper market

In this chapter you will learn:
- why the newspaper market is a match for the beginner
- how to approach newspaper editors
- secrets of syndication!

The three basic market categories for the travel piece are: books, magazines and newspapers. While the book market is primarily reserved for the more experienced travel writer and the magazine market for the journalist with one or two clips, the newspaper arena is wide open for the newcomer.

Newspapers come in all shapes and sizes. These periodicals include community papers, published weekly or biweekly, with a length of as few as ten pages and a front page covering topics like the local beauty pageant or last night's school football game. On the other end of the spectrum are internationally-recognized dailies like the *New York Times* and the *Times of London*. But the one entity all these newspapers have in common is readers who travel.

Newspaper travel feature

Most small-town papers run a regular travel feature and dailies in large, urban centres have a separate weekly travel section (usually Sunday). Logic tells you it is easier to get published by the smaller tabloid. But even larger newspapers that don't buy much from freelancers do buy travel pieces. Why? It's less expensive to pay an independent for a piece about a foreign destination than to send a staff member to the other side of the world to cover the same topic.

The criteria are simple:

- cover a destination of interest to the paper's readers
- provide clear but arresting copy
- be objective
- resist the flowery, abundant-adjective approach
- include up-to-date, accurate facts
- supplement the piece with a variety of luring photographs.

Another key is to study several back issues of the newspaper's travel section and write articles similar in length, noting whether the pieces are written in first person (I), second person (you) or the most commonly-used third person (he or she). The more compatible the piece is with the feel of the paper, the better chance there is for publication.

The newspaper scoop

The downside to the newspaper market is low pay. *Writer's Market* shows the following pay scale for the newspaper market. Feature: US $25 low, US $200 mid-range, US $500 high/piece, depending on circulation. In Canada, 15–40 cents/word, but rates vary widely.

Entry into the newspaper market is easier for a novice writer, however. Magazines lean more toward the published writer, usually requiring a query and clips from previously printed pieces. Newspapers do not. And an added bonus is that once newspaper travel pieces are published, the writer has clips.

Author guidelines

Before you approach a newspaper with a travel article, it's wise to ask if they have author or writer's guidelines. Most larger periodicals do and eagerly provide them to interested journalists who make the request with an SAE. (Some newspapers respond to on-line requests and transmit guidelines via e-mail.)

Written by editors, these guidelines (see the following table) tell you exactly what they are looking for: editorial concept, story length, pay and like information. (*Note*: Indicate on these guidelines the date they were received. You'll appreciate this notation at a later date when you refer to these written tips and wonder if they are current.)

Author guidelines

The Miami Herald
Quick Trips – Author Guidelines

Quick Trips are stories about destinations that can be visited from South Florida in a couple of days. These stories should evoke ambience and a sense of why someone would want to go there. They also should be extremely useful, with specific recommendations for lodgings, activities and dining. Quick Trips can be oriented toward a certain audience: the family guide to Key West versus the couples' guide to Key West, for instance, or be general.

Here are the details:

- **Length:** 25–30 inches, plus sidebars. (The longer the sidebars, the shorter the main.)

- **Trip planner:** This box should help readers figure out quickly if this trip is for them. It should include the following information:
  - **Best for:** Who is this trip best for? History lovers? Nature lovers? Families? Couples? Gay couples?
  - **Also good for:** Secondary groups.
  - **Cost for a two-night visit in (qualify the type of accommodation):** Think typical accommodation here; if this is a place known for its historic accommodation, price it for the historic accommodation. Include what someone might reasonably spend on meals, etc. Again, think type. We might say that a budget weekend in this place costs US $250 for two people; weekend in historic accommodation with visits to fine restaurants costs US $600.
  - **Highlights:** Just list the things someone shouldn't miss; include more detail on them in your story.
  - **Special events:** The two–five major festivals each year, with dates.
  - **Getting there:** Drive time, or fly time, from South Florida. (Use the one most likely; for instance, one can drive to Key West, but one wouldn't if one lived in South Florida.) If flying is involved, tell us who goes there ('several major airlines' will do fine if that is the case, but be sure to include any discount airlines such as Air Tran, Southwest or Delta Express).
  - **Information:** Contact info for the destination; be sure to include Web address.
- **Lodging recommendations:** All Quick Trips must include a box with recommendations for lodgings that the writer has actually visited. At least five lodgings should be included; they should include budget, moderate and luxury options. Brief descriptions of the hotels, plus rates, must be included.
- **Dining recommendations:** Requirements here are less stringent. One way to get these is to ask a knowledgeable local what they recommend and quote them as the source. (Jane Doe, owner of the Mill House Inn, recommends these four restaurants: A, B, C and D.)

(It is also noted in the general travel section guidelines of *The Miami Herald* that payment is made on publication and rates range from US $150 for a normal-length article, US $25 for black and white photographs and US $75 for colour photographs.)

More guidance

Some newspapers provide additional guidance beyond the guidelines. While the following tips from *The Dallas Morning News* were authored to give insight into that particular periodical's criteria, the advice is of value to any travel writer.

What We're Looking For: Below are some hints on writing travel stories for us. We don't discourage different approaches and styles, though a simple, straightforward narrative usually is best. Be specific, precise and factual. Tell a good story.

No P.R. please: We give priority to stories based on unsponsored trips. Avoid promoting a particular business, hotel, resort. We are looking for consumer information, not adjective-laden copy.

The adjective disease: Avoid cliched descriptions and adjective overload. Don't tell us something is beautiful – tell us why it's beautiful. We are tired of 'majestic' mountains, 'spectacular' canyons, 'quaint' villages, and 'charming' hamlets.

Get close: Details are what make an experience real for readers. Focus on specifics that illustrate the whole. This often is true of photos, too. Crowds can be boring; people seldom are.

Talk to people: Bring a place to life with its inhabitants. Use relevant quotes and anecdotes.

I scream, we scream: First-person is OK, though not crucial. If there is a 'we' in your story, explain who the other person or people are.

Surprise us: Give us something new, something out of the ordinary. Tell us what you did or saw that was unique, that only someone who was there would know.

Act up: Be a reporter, not a passive observer walking us through a brochure or guidebook. Don't regurgitate journal entries. Meet people, try things, get involved.

Past mastery: The history of a destination is important but usually secondary. Keep it brief. There are exceptions. Sometimes the history is the story. In that case, you need to make it come to life. Anecdotes and quotes are particularly important.

Good, bad, and ugly: Don't sugar-coat an experience or a location. The hassles are important information, too. Often the most memorable travel experiences are those that, at the time, were trying.

Request annual editorial calendars

Don't guess when each newspaper is concentrating on Latin America or Alaska or any other destination. Find out. One easy way to accomplish this is an end-of-the-year assignment. In October or so, request the following year's editorial calendar for the travel section. Or contact the publication's advertising department and ask for the travel section's advertising schedule, not mentioning that you're a travel writer.

The last suggestion may provide you with the most valuable information. Thinking you're a potential advertiser, the newspaper will include not only the editorial calendar but specific travel demographics about its readers as well.

Say the demographic research indicates 38% of a publication's readership annually visit Hawaii and 71% of its audience are women. With this information, approach the newspaper with a Hawaii piece or maybe a spa feature; and refer to the statistics: 'As 38% of your readers visit Hawaii each year, you may be interested in my 1500-word article on Maui's famed road to Hana', you might write. Or say this: 'I am confident my 1200-word piece entitled 'America's Top 10 Spas' would be of particular interest to 71% of your readers – the women.'

Peruse these editorial calendars, note the topics that interest you, make a master calendar and refer to this reference piece when making submissions. Your calendar notations might be: January 7, adventure travel, *Chicago Tribune*; January 21, spa vacations, *Toronto Star*; February 4, fall/winter cruises, *Sydney Morning Herald*.

The suggested calendar will help you organize. But, more important, it serves to minimize rejections. Think about it. If your article on Acapulco is timed to coincide with the newspaper's upcoming Mexico section, you've increased your odds for publication. You've demonstrated you know more about the periodical than simply its name and address.

Newspaper database

Develop your own database of potential newspaper markets. You might ask how to find major newspapers. You can use a variety of library references including *Gale Directory of Publications and Broadcast Media,* the *Working Press of the Nation, Literary Market Place* or *International Literary Market Place.* (See the references section at the end of the book.) Use the librarian's guidance to find the reference work suited to your individual needs.

My alphabetical newspaper list has information including addresses, telephone numbers and travel editors' names (if available). I update this list annually. It includes dated notations like 'Accepting no freelance – 11/01', 'Uses no articles from sponsored trips – 3/02', or 'No first-person pieces – 1/03'.

Because of editor turnover, it's advisable to call the newspaper or pull its Web site to double-check the name, spelling and sometimes gender (in names like Leslie Blakely) of the travel editor before making a submission. In instances when this clarification process entails the expense of an international call, you may want to replace a name with the title *travel editor.*

Multiple submissions

One way to maximize your sales is to submit an article with national appeal to several regional newspapers whose circulation areas do not overlap (within a 100-mile radius of one another). For example, circulation areas of *The San Diego Union-Tribune* and *The Los Angeles Times* overlap, just as the *Toronto Times* and *Toronto Sun* do. Conversely, multiple submissions to papers in UK cities such as Belfast, Edinburgh or Birmingham are perfectly acceptable.

It is important, however, to note that multiple submissions are not possible with newspapers that have national circulations like the *New York Times* and the *Wall Street Journal.* A national publication wants exclusive national rights. This means you can't sell to more than one of them, or to any of them and to regional newspapers at the same time.

Here's how you make multiple submissions. Send a manuscript to each newspaper travel editor, with a cover letter indicating the work is 'exclusive in your circulation area'. This wording means you are not offering the same piece to the city's competing daily or to any newspaper distributed in the same market. But if the editor of *The Boston Globe* returns the manuscript unused, immediately send it to the *Boston Herald* – because you're no longer competing.

To keep track of your submissions, prepare a distribution sheet for each article with the following: publications contacted, date of submission, response, date of response and other pertinent information (see the following table).

Sample article distribution list
Australia down-under *dos*

Newspaper	Date	Ms	Pics	SAE	Response	Response date
S.F. Chronicle	5/02	X	X	X	Yes	6/02
Dallas M. News	5/02	X	X	X	No	7/02
Denver Post	6/02	X	X	X	No	6/02 Just did similar
Chicago Sun	6/02	X	X	X	No	6/02 No, but try again
Miami Herald	6/02	X	X	X	Yes	7/02
Seattle Times	7/02	X	X	X	Yes	7/02
Chicago Tribune	7/02	X	X	X	Yes	7/02

I staple the distribution sheet on the inside of the file folder containing the article, research, contact names, expenses; and if accepted and published, a copy of the contract, clips and payment stub. This method should be followed for all submissions (both newspaper and magazine).

When this multiple strategy works for you, your pay multiplies as well. Thus one newspaper article accepted by four publications (with an average rate of US $100–150) can generate income between US $400–600.

Freelance friendly?

Analyze a newspaper's travel section. Look at the articles' bylines. Does it say The Associated Press under the author's name? Staff writer? *Los Angeles Daily News?* Any of these notations tell you these articles were not purchased from freelancers.

Tag lines like 'Erin Marie is a freelance writer based in Davis, California' or 'Freelancer Kathryn Lane makes her home in London, England' give the green light to freelancers.

Syndicates

Most travel writers dream of having their work distributed to newspapers or magazines across the country – even around the world; they dream of becoming syndicated. This goal, however, is not an easy one to achieve.

The first step toward syndication is to understand it. (See Words of writing wisdom at the end of this chapter.) Syndicates disburse your articles, with the profits split between you and the syndicate. Most syndicated columnists begin by writing for local newspapers, thus developing a collection of clips. But it doesn't stop there.

This column must showcase a new idea and one that is appropriate for the intended syndication. The idea must also be one that doesn't compete with a column already in print or on a subject the syndicate already covers. Next analyze the work of well-known, popular columnists. Learn from it, but don't try to duplicate it. The key is to produce a column that is yours alone, has unique appeal, is reflective of today's trends and that will sell.

The following steps should be familiar by now. Select a syndicate to approach, request a copy of its writer's guidelines and follow up with an attractive syndication package including a query letter, five or six columns and an SAE.

Try to sell a column idea on your own. Then once your column is featured in a few papers, put a package together of these samples. Don't underestimate the value of this package as a selling piece. It demonstrates that an established market is already in place for your work.

Clip clues

'It's the old cart-horse thing', says travel writer Katharine Dyson:

Before most editors will even look at your work, they want to see clips of what you have already published. But how can you supply these if no one will publish what you have written?

My advice: contact local publishers and newspapers with a story idea. Use all the contacts you can draw on. Call them and follow up with a letter. Then call them again. And don't be disappointed if you hear nothing.

Editors mean well, but are generally overworked and have little time to work with writers they don't know. I used to get a dozen or so inquiries each week when I was editor and they piled up. But keep writing. And trying. Eventually, if you stay with it, someone, somewhere will print your work if your writing is any good.

Once you have several published articles in hand, start a portfolio to display your work. While most editors automatically send you tear sheets of your stories, you may need to request them. And for major stories, ask for several. Your clip book showcases your professionalism. It's a valuable tool to show editors when seeking additional assignments and when approaching new markets.

Xeroxed copies of clips (never send originals) are important to provide to public relations executives or world tourist organizations when seeking assistance with free or reduced-rate travel or accommodation. Tear sheets are also used when applying for membership in most writers' associations.

Words of writing wisdom
... for syndication

With more than 15 years' experience, Pamela Stone has had freelance articles distributed by the New York Times and the Los Angeles Times Syndicates, appearing in: *Chicago Tribune, Los Angeles Times, Baltimore Sun, Detroit News and Free Press, Rocky Mountain News, Boston Globe* and the *Palm Beach Post,* among others nationally.

Most journalists are faced with one great fear: you are only as good as your last article. After endless hours of research, interviewing and travel, it's important to get the most mileage out of your pieces. That's why it's key for writers to resell their material.

Whether you are interested in reselling to national syndicates or through self-syndication, it's important that you write for the masses. Make sure your piece is properly positioned to a target market, then pitch it appropriately to an editor who will place the story.

The three main elements are position, pitch and place. Here's how it works:

1 Study, study, study the market: *Read, read, read up to five newspapers and news magazines a day like* New York Times, USA TODAY, Wall Street Journal, *your local newspaper,* Time, Newsweek, *or other publications like* Talk, Rolling Stone, Esquire *or* Vanity Fair, *etc. Also,* American Demographics *is a great magazine for addressing issues, trends and demographic changes affecting the populace.*

   If you're writing features, for instance, it's important that you become aware of common trends that affect the country. If you're writing a business or travel story, you may change your reading material, but the principle remains the same.

2 Position: *The easiest way to position your idea in the marketplace is through your title. Study titles of articles in popular magazines, like* Redbook, Family Circle, Oxygen *or even* Businessweek. *The title of your article must reflect the theme of your idea. It must grab the reader's attention. It must evoke an emotional response. In short, it must sell, sell, sell!*

3 Pitch your idea: *Study news or magazine publications, places where you want to pitch the idea. Who is their target market? Who reads the publication and why? How do you find out this information? Call the marketing department. Tell them you're a marketing student at your local university. Or tell them you work for an advertising agency.*

   Ask them to send you a media kit for their publication. Ask for the demographics the publication is trying to reach. Is your idea a good match for the publication? If it's a newspaper, decide which section your idea fits into. Then, get the name of the editor and contact him/her appropriately.

4 Place: *Once you have your idea and pitch well developed, then you can try to place it. Now you're ready to write pitch letters or query the news publications. But, you must research which syndicates you want to reach. Study*

Bacon's Newspaper Directory – *it lists the syndicates. You can also surf the Net to find sites that match your needs.*

5 To syndicate or not?*: Whether you self-syndicate or have your article(s) syndicated nationally, you must make sure your article meets the needs and interests of the masses. It must address a national trend. It may concern political corruption that's sweeping the nation, failed marriages, caregiving, leaving children home alone, teen pregnancies, travel arrangements made via Internet, or more.*

6 Appeal*: In order for the* New York Times *or* Los Angeles Times *Syndicates or Knight Ridder/Tribune Information Service to pick up an article or one-shot, the idea must have on-going appeal. For reselling the article to other newspapers throughout the country, they get one-half of the fee, which ranges from US $75–$350.*

7 Tenacity*: Don't give up. More than any other profession, syndicating articles has to do with pushing the envelope. Success is found in innovative but salesworthy ideas. It takes an insatiable curiosity, guts and a go-get-em attitude.*

06
selling to magazines

In this chapter you will learn:
- how to analyse a magazine
- the value of writer's guidelines
- insight into publishing rights.

Magazines are the best market for travel articles. They pay more and they're more prestigious. When many people hear the word *magazine*, they think in terms of a national glossy consumer publication like *Conde Nast Traveler British Edition*.

But the magazine market is loaded with local and regional possibilities having names like *Ann Arbor Observer* (Ann Arbor, Michigan) and *The Country Connection* (Boulter, Ontario). Then there are in-flight magazines, trade publications and more.

Types of magazines

First of all, there are city and regional publications. The benefit of writing about locations close to home is two-fold; you're writing about and photographing what you know and you're acquiring clips at a minimum expense. As a local writer, you have an advantage over the out-of-town journalist in terms of value to an editor. You know the area intimately.

Then there are specialty magazines. Inexperienced travel writers err by contacting only magazines specializing in travel. Other consumer publications worth investigating include:

- adventure, outdoor sports, recreation
- bridal
- food and drink
- historical
- nature and natural history
- women's magazines.

Types of pieces that could be submitted to these types of publications might have names like 'Sundance Ski Resort', 'Honeymoon on St Barts', or 'Travel Solo/Travel Safely' and so on.

Next come in-flight, in-room and auto club members' magazines. Most major airlines provide magazines for their passengers to read during the flight. Articles cover the airlines' destinations and general interests. The target market for these monthlies is the business traveller and leisure vacationer.

Some major hotel chains provide similar reading material for guests called in-room magazines. These publications may be monthly, bimonthly, tri-monthly, even quarterly; and travel-related stories cover destinations where the hotel chain has properties.

Auto club members' magazines are distributed to the club membership, which can represent a circulation in the millions. These publications focus on auto news, driving trips, national and international destinations, cruise travel and tours. (See the first Words of writing wisdom at the end of this chapter.)

Don't forget trade publications – this type of periodical represents a little known market to writers who rely exclusively on those popular consumer publications that crowd the shelves of newsstands and bookstores. Yet it is an excellent market for writers, especially the inexperienced writer.

Writer's Market says:

> Writers who have discovered trade journals have found a market that offers the chance to publish regularly in subject areas they find interesting, editors who are typically more accessible than their commercial counterparts and pay rates that rival those of the big-name magazines.
>
> *Writer's Market,* 1999

Advice to the newcomer approaching a trade magazine editor is to mention first-hand knowledge you have of the respective industry in your query or cover letter. If you query a convention/incentive meetings magazine, for example, and have experience as a meeting planner, tell the editor. Likewise, a former travel agent should include this credential in correspondence to a travel trade magazine. (See the second Words of writing wisdom at the end of this chapter.)

Study marketing manuals

Marketing tools like annual editions of *Writer's Market*, *International Writers' & Artists' Yearbook* (British counterpart of *Writer's Market*), *Literary Market Place* and *International Literary Market Place* are designed to assist the freelancer in deciding where and how to submit articles. (Note that some of these publications are available on CD-ROM.) Each of these reference books varies slightly but for the purpose of simplification, the *Writer's Market* will be covered in this chapter.

As you would with any book, look at the table of contents first. You'll note the three largest sections of *Writer's Market* are listings of book publishers, consumer magazines and trade, technical and professional journals. Additional topics include syndicates, a glossary and writing-related Web sites.

Study the specific markets within these categories, identifying those that have potential for the travel writer. Let's walk through the process. Within the consumer market are obvious possibilities: travel, camping and trailer; general interest and in-flight.

But beyond these apparent categories are other magazine possibilities. Following is a short list of these markets and a sample travel topic which might interest each of them: art and architecture (the pyramids – Egypt's architectural feat), childcare and parental guidance (car travel with a toddler), disabilities (cruise ships for the wheelchair-bound traveller), food and drink (five of Ireland's most popular potato dishes), health & fitness (climbing Mt Ranier), juvenile (successful teen travel with mum and dad), men (discovering the island of Jersey by bike), military (Annapolis' naval academy) and religious (a visit to Portugal's Fatima). When studying the markets take note: lower profile and less obvious markets often represent the best opportunities.

Now evaluate individual listings. Pay attention to the location of the publication, the types of material it wants to see, submission requirements, rights and payment policies. Each of these items can be a deciding factor for the journalist.

Let's analyze a fictitious publication as it would appear in *Writer's Market*. (Note that key information appears in bold.)

$$$$ *Westward Ho!, The Magazine for Washington, Oregon and California.* Address. Telephone number. Fax number. E-mail address. Editor-in-Chief: (Name). **Contact:** (Name). **80% freelance written.** '*Westward Ho!* is a bimonthly magazine for West Coast residents. It publishes travel, automobile-related, lifestyle, culture and history features by writers from a variety of disciplines and includes destinations in the US and internationally.' Estab. 1925. Circ. 800,000. **Pays on acceptance.** Byline given. Buys first rights. Offers 25–50% kill fee. Submit seasonal material 18 months in advance. Reports in 3 months on queries; 2 weeks on assigned mss. Sample copy for $6. Writer's guidelines for SAE.

Non-fiction: Annual great drives, travel and art, family travel and cruising themes issues. Destination stories based on a writer's single trip to the place described. **Buys 50 mss/year.** Query with published clips. *No unsolicited mss.* Length: 600–2500 words. **Pays 50 cents [US] – $1/word.** Pays the expenses of writers on assignment.

Photos: 'Freelancers should not concern themselves with photography. We assign professional photographers.'

Columns/departments: Week Ends (weekend travel in Washington, Oregon and California), 1500 words; Good Sports (outdoor recreation), 1700 words; Food Souvenirs (memoir and recipe from Western travel), 400 words plus recipe. Buys 30 mss/year. Query with published clips. **Pays 50 cents/word.**

Tips: 'We are most interested in writers with a special expertise to bring to the travel experience, i.e., architecture, theatre, snowboarding, etc.'

This listing imparted valuable information about *Westward Ho!*:

1 distributes to the Washington, Oregon and California market
2 publishes travel
3 covers US and international destinations
4 pays on acceptance (POA) rather than on publication (POP)
5 provides good freelance possibilities (80% freelance written)
6 wants query with published clips
7 does not want unsolicited manuscripts
8 pays well (50 cents–US $1/word)
9 does not expect photography.

The *tip* notation in any listing can provide the most critical information. The following are tips given by three different magazines in *Writer's Market:* 'We do not like to receive queries via fax or e-mail unless the writer does not expect a reply'; '*Conde Nast Traveler* tells us that they are no longer accepting unsolicited submissions'; 'Be professional. Use a word processor'.

Dissect the magazine

When submitting to a magazine, study the market. Request a sample copy and analyze the publication. Start with its look. Is it a four-colour glossy or a news print tabloid? Your answer will tell you what kind of cheque to expect. The rule of thumb is: the richer the look, the better the pay.

Look at the advertising. Is it abundant with ads like Mercedes-Benz, Tiffany and Seabourn Cruise Line? Or are advertisements aimed at the consumers of McDonalds and Budget Car Rental? The implications of these ads tell volumes about the magazine's readers.

They tell the savvy travel writer whether to submit an article entitled 'Bangkok on a Budget' or 'Luxurious London'. This invaluable exercise gives the travel writer an insight into the publication's patrons. It tells you who the readers are and how a piece can be geared to these readers.

Study the masthead next. Usually found in the first few pages of the magazine, the masthead contains names of editors, staffers and contributors. Match these names with the bylines on the articles. If non-staffers are non-existent on the list, assume the publication buys little freelance.

Look at the names of the freelancers. Are they high-profile ones? For example, is there an article penned by Madonna on London (her new home) or did Julia Child author a piece on Thanksgiving dinner in New England? If so, you need to evaluate the importance of the celebrity credential with this publication.

Study the length of the articles. Do they average 2500 words or are they no longer than 1000 words? If the publication accepts only 800-word pieces, you'll be out of luck if you try to sell a 3000-word story in your query letter.

Continue your exploration. Are the travel stories local, regional, national, North American, European or worldwide? Look at how these places are covered: destination piece, specialty aspect (shopping, dining, etc.), seasonal angle. This bit of sleuth work can tell you whether a piece should be submitted on Cairo's exotic bazaar market or the local farmers' market.

Are there sidebars? If so, do they provide hard facts or whimsical asides? Do they use photographs or artwork? Is photography in colour or black and white? Look at the verbiage. Is the sentence structure short and snappy or lengthy and flowery? What about the tone – formal or conversational? Are foreign phrases used for flavour? How about quotes? All this information will help you compose an effective query and write a subsequent article that will sell.

Writer's guidelines

Just as you prepare to approach the newspaper market by requesting author or writer's guidelines, so should you with the magazine market. Following are writer's guidelines from *Travel & Leisure*. Many of the tips shared by this editorial staff can serve the freelancer well when approaching most high-profile publications.

Writer Guidelines

Travel & Leisure is monthly and has a circulation of over 1,000,000 subscribers, plus limited newsstand distribution. Our readers are sophisticated, active travelers who look to us for planning both pleasure and business trips.

About 95 percent of the magazine is written by freelance writers on assignment. Every assignment is confirmed by a contract. We buy only the first-time world rights, and request that the work not be published elsewhere until 90 days after it appears in T+L. We pay upon acceptance of the article. Neither editors nor contributors may accept free travel.

How to Proceed:

1 Look at several issues of the magazine and become familiar with the types of articles published in the various sections, and the two Regional editions, whose page numbers carry letters that indicate the region – E (East), W (West).

2 Please note that a piece is not an idea, and that editors are looking for a compelling reason to assign an article: a specific angle, news that makes the subject fresh, a writer's enthusiasm for and familiarity with the topic.

3 Service information is important to every destination article: when to go, how to get there, where to stay, where to eat, what to see and do. The reader must be able to follow in the author's footsteps, and the articles are scheduled with that in mind – i.e., before the season in question. We have a three-month lead time.

4 Please do not telephone us about story proposals. Instead send a query letter that briefly outlines the ideas (no more than three at once) being proposed. Please enclose recent clips of your work and a SASE [SAE]. Query letters can also be via e-mail. The address is Tlquery@amexpub.com. In most cases, e-mail queries will receive the fastest responses.

5 It is rare that we will assign a feature article to a writer with whom we have not worked. The best section to start with are departments in the front and back of the magazine and the regional editions.

Guidelines give you the insider's look at a publication and its needs. And just as periodicals vary; guidelines vary. Following are tips culled from three uniquely different magazines.

Golf & Travel magazine:

Golf & Travel aims to provide its readers with uncommon golf stories. We are interested in writers who can combine the two subjects of golf and travel with a third element that is not easily named but has to do with a sophisticated tone, an intelligent attitude, a sensitive eye and, where appropriate, a sense of humor or irony.

Islands magazine:

Islands is a travel magazine that focuses on islands around the world: urban, rural, tropical or windswept, well-known or virtually undiscovered. We strive for geographical and topical diversity and encourage articles with a well-defined focus and point of view. Our purpose is, in effect, to take the reader to the island. To that end, we seek informative, insightful, personal pieces that reveal the essence of the place.

Spa magazine:

Your article will probably require research and interviews with experts – and in many cases, you'll be expected to experience whatever treatment or spa you are covering. Because our magazine is service oriented, most pieces are written in second person ('you'), using an active voice whenever possible. Scholarly third-person articles and the passive voice are best left to college term papers. The idea is to take readers through the experience you are covering – whether it's a sneak peek at a hip new spa or doing a home pedicure.

Finding more markets

Keep in mind that while you might consider a publication like *Writer's Market* (listing over 8000 editors in its 2003 edition) your Bible, so do most travel writers. For this reason, it's important to look beyond obvious resources to beat the competition.

One such resource is *Travelwriter Marketletter*, a monthly newsletter exclusively devoted to many known and little-known travel-friendly publications. This fact-filled ten-page periodical, available by subscription (www.travelwriterml.com), has entries like the following:

ActiveTimes *is a quarterly newspaper magazine covering the over-50 market. Editor Chris Kelly wants articles on positive, enjoyable aspects of aging. Wants travel roundups, but not destinations. Circulation is five million. Pay is usually 50 cents a word, rarely [US]$1, on publication, for 1st NA serial [First North American Serial Rights] and electronic reprint rights. Guidelines and sample issue for 9 × 12 SASE [SAE]. 417 Main St., Carbondale, CO 81623.*

But good old-fashioned leg work shouldn't be overlooked. Collect obscure magazines like throw-away publications and association magazines. Ask your doctors' offices, hair salons and friends to save old periodicals for you. Regularly peruse newsstand and bookstore shelves for new magazines. Save any and all in-flight magazines. Take home magazines from the theatre. Pick up foreign publications when on the road. Each of these periodicals represent a potential new market.

Develop a database

Put your knowledge of magazine markets to use and develop a database of possibilities. Input the information culled from resources such as *Writer's Market, International Writers' & Artists' Yearbook* and newsletters like *Travelwriter Marketletter*. Add the names and pertinent information for newly discovered publications. But for the database to have significant value as a reference when making a submission list, it must be updated frequently and include viable magazines (not *every* magazine).

Simultaneous submissions

As admitted earlier, I'm a professed writing class junkie. Although it was years ago, I still recall my first class and the instructor's warning not to submit to more than one national magazine at a time. Thus, I would carefully prepare a query and mail it to my first choice magazine. And I'd wait. One, two, maybe three months. If the response was no, I then mailed the query and clips to my second choice. Get the picture?

Then I came across a spunky instructor with different advice. Eva Shaw, author of more than 1000 magazine articles and over 35 published books, proclaimed my one-query-at-a-time rule as out of date and out of touch with the real world of publishing. I think her actual words were: 'Cynthia, grow up.' And she's right.

Travel writing is your job. You do it to make money. Editors understand that. The next logical question is: 'What if more than one magazine wants the article?' What a problem to have!

Eva Shaw's advice in *The Successful Writer's Guide to Publishing Magazine Articles* (Rodgers & Nelsen Publishing Co.) is this:

> *Choose the magazine that will do the most for your career, has the most potential for additional sales or, of course, offers the most money.*

> *But what should you do with the second or third positive reply? Be honest. Write or call the editor, explain that you've just spoken to another editor and the idea was snapped up. However, you happen to have another sterling topic. Then explain it. Or write or call the editor and offer the same topic with another irresistible slant.*

Lead time

The amount of time between the submission of the article and the date of publication is called the lead time. For newspapers this time may be as little as a few weeks, but for magazines, it's substantially longer and it varies from publication to publication. For example, the lead time for *AAA Today* is 12 months, compared to a 6-month lead time for *Spa*.

The lead time is a significant factor to consider when submitting seasonal pieces like 'A Hawaiian Christmas' or 'Ski the

Rockies'. And it's important to note that a publication's seasonal lead time is many times longer than its editorial lead time.

Recycle/reslant/resell

'In order to make it in the freelance world, it's important to stretch your article as far as possible', says author Pamela Stone:

> *Article spin-offs are the meat of all freelancers. Make the most of your research and time. In my case, I interviewed countless women who were learning to live alone.*
>
> *Then, I wrote several articles on the subject, including 'Making Your Money Matter', 'Solo Parenting', 'Say No and Mean It', 'Cutting the Ties', and 'Learning to Let Go'. These articles were incorporated into my self-help book called* A Woman's Guide to Living Alone: 10 Ways to Survive Grief and Be Happy *(Taylor Publishing, 2001).*

This advice can easily be applied to the travel writing arena. Many times you will have far more material – solid facts, colourful anecdotes, local tidbits – than you can use in one article. These are the times to rework or reslant the material into several pieces.

A portion of the basic destination information will be reused but the end result will be three or four new pieces – each with a different focus, title, beginning and ending. Sometimes it may be years later that travel material is expanded into a new piece. In these instances, of course, use only timeless information that can be enhanced with up-to-date facts.

Recycling previously published pieces (unless you sold all rights) is an excellent way to increase your income. If you have sold first rights (see publishing rights section), you are free to resell your work once it has appeared. What is the procedure? Accompany the manuscript (not a clip or photocopy of the piece as it appeared in another publication) with a cover letter detailing where and when the piece originally appeared. Expect half to two-thirds of the original fee.

This is a relatively labour free, inexpensive method to expand into other markets – regional, national and international. Thus, for the minimum effort and expense of reprinting pieces, composing cover letters, adding clips of other work, addressing envelopes and driving to the postal office, the payoff can be additional sales. But the prime benefit is that incalculable advantage called *exposure*.

Back-of-the-book stories

Articles appearing on pages numbered oddly like C71/2 and D80/2 and never listed in the table of contents are typically called back-of-the-book stories. The name is deceiving – the pieces may appear in the front or the middle; they aren't necessarily located at the back of the publication. But as *Travel & Leisure* suggests in its guidelines, it's a good place to begin.

Publishing rights

As a writer it's important for you to understand what rights you are selling when you agree to have your work published. The general rule of thumb is the more rights you sell, the more you should be paid and the less control you retain.

Following are the more important standard categories of rights for publishing in newspapers and magazines. (Book rights are covered by the contract between the writer and the book publisher.)

First serial rights

If you sell first serial rights to a newspaper or magazine, you are selling the right to publish the piece for the first time. All other rights to the material remain with the writer. Geographical limits are often specified with first serial rights. Example: First North American serial rights means, quite literally, that it hasn't appeared previously in North America.

Second serial (or reprint) rights

Relinquishing this publishing right gives a newspaper or magazine the right to print an article after it has appeared in another publication. Second serial rights are not limited to reselling the article only twice. It may be for a third, fourth or fifth time and so on.

One-time rights

The sell of one-time rights means giving a magazine or newspaper the permission to publish the article once, irrespective of priority. Thus, there is nothing to stop the author from selling the work to other publications at the same time. (Note: These simultaneous sales should not be to publications with overlapping circulations or audiences.)

All rights

If you sell all rights, you forgo the right ever to use your work again. Thus, licencing away all rights means you can no longer sell your work as the basis for a movie, translate and publish it in other languages, include it on a cassette recording or an electronic information network, reprint, adapt or resell it anywhere. You don't even retain the right to use a substantial portion of your own material in a book you may later write.

Electronic rights

These rights cover usage in a broad range of electronic media. Contracts should specify if, and which, electronic rights are included.

What about money?

According to *Writer's Market* the magazine pay scale is: feature articles – anywhere from 20 cents to US $4/word; or US $150–$2750 for a 1500-word article, depending on size (circulation) and reputation of magazine.

Magazine column – 25 cents low, US $1.50 mid-range, US $4 high/word; US $25 low, US $2500 high/piece. Larger circulation publications pay fees related to their regular word rate.

Alternative market advice

Beyond newspapers and magazines are alternative markets: advertorials, regular columns, syndicates, international publications, travel brochures, press releases (travel-related subjects), slide show/video scripts and seminars/workshops.

Katharine Dyson has successfully tapped a number of these travel writing options:

> *When you see the amount of brochures and other pieces of mail that come into your home, you realize that anyone*

who has a programme or product to sell, needs someone who can write their message clearly.

When I first entered the freelance field 10 years ago, I decided to tap into that market. Even though I did not yet have a computer, I sent out letters to tourism boards, tour operators, travel agents and others in the industry offering my services for articles as well as advertorials, brochures and newsletters.

One reply led to an ongoing commitment to write, design and produce the newsletter for the German National Tourist Office, a bimonthly job that lasted for three years. With this guaranteed source of steady income, I was able to purchase a computer and printer.

In addition to producing the newsletter, I queried other publications acquiring other work including a biweekly travel column in a group of area newspapers, writing a newsletter for Virgin Atlantic Airways and Tradesco Tours, a brochure for Expo Garden Tours and a customized newsletter for travel agents.

Advertorials

Advertorial, as the name suggests, is the combination of an advertisement and an editorial. While the piece may look and often sound like a editorial, the word *advertisement* is notated on each page. The biggest difference between an advertorial and a traditional travel article is that an advertorial must be positive, as opposed to an article, which is objective.

Suggestions for these pieces originate at the publication – you don't query a magazine with a great advertorial idea. And assignments for the pieces are generally made by the sales, advertising or promotion department. As listed in *Writer's Market*, pay is US $650 low, US $1000 high/printed page.

Regular column

Regular columns appear in every newspaper and magazine – small or large, local or national. The best entry into this field is probably through the community newspaper or magazine door, with a column on topics like 'weekend trips' or 'travel-related questions and answers'. Once established in a smaller market, the travel writer is now armed with clips of a regular travel column and can approach a larger market.

Words of writing wisdom

... from a members' magazine

Tom Wuckovich is the senior editor for *AAA Going Places* magazine, a 2.3-million circulation travel publication for AAA members in Florida, Georgia and Tennessee. He has also written for a number of travel magazines and newspaper travel sections.

Obviously I've been approached many times about submissions for Going Places *magazine – both by freelancers and staff writers/editors who also freelance. What gets my attention, and ultimately acceptance of an article could be quite different than other editors in my position, but here are some general guidelines:*

- *I prefer to see an article rather than a query because simply by reading the lead, I can determine if the quality of writing is suitable for publication.*

- *I almost always reject articles about the states we circulate in since we usually can, and do, send staff to cover these destinations. The story would have to be very unusual to cross this hurdle.*

- *Letters or phone calls are fine, but be certain you are familiar with our magazine before you attempt to pitch a story idea. Knowing our market and our purpose will also help you narrow your focus.*

- *Send a manuscript that is professional in every respect – especially check the spelling. Sounds simple, but I can't tell you how many I receive with misspellings. Include captions for artwork – and good artwork is a plus.*

- *We don't make assignments. But you should know that if you did your homework on our publication.*

- *Be patient, and don't press about when a story will run. If the material is time sensitive, say so, but that doesn't necessarily mean we will run it. The fact that we are interested is a good sign and might lead to other articles. We like to use writers we become familiar with and trust.*

- *I tend to open mail that is handwritten, rather than typed.*

  All these things weigh in my decision, but there is no substitute for good writing.

Words of writing wisdom

... from the trades

Leesa Witty is former managing editor for three US travel trade publications, *Meetings West*, *Meetings South* and *Meetings East*. She began her career as a freelance journalist.

As an editor, the first thing I look for in a pitched story is whether or not it is a fit for our audience. A freelance writer cannot write an article or come up with an idea and pitch it to every magazine that it may fit. For example, a writer may have a piece on Maui and believe that any travel publication would be interested in buying it. That is not true. Travel magazines have different focuses, different angles and different audiences. First and foremost, know the audience for the magazine you are pitching.

From there, if the article seems to fit with our readership, I look at the angle. Out-of-the-box thinking and unique article ideas always get my second glance. Our readers are looking for new information and new articles, so I'm looking for that unique angle on a story that no one else has pitched or that isn't common. Many people have written that spas are great and they are a new trend. Or that New Orleans is a party town for every age. I am looking for angles that take a little deeper look at places.

It goes without saying that I am looking for good writing. As an editor, it is my job to clean up an article and tweak it to our fit. Good writing helps, but I'm more interested in the unique story angle.

Lastly and very importantly, I look for writers who are available when I need them. Especially around deadline times when I may have questions about a person's name, the spelling of a city or similar details. I need the writer to be available to finish the article at this time – to follow through with questions and suggestions. These qualities absolutely would put a writer at the top of my freelance list.

07

development of an article

To many, travel writing is straightforward. It's the colourful rendition of a journey. A travel article gives a sense of place, boosts interest and tells the reader what to do, when to go, where to eat, where to stay and how to get there. Some feel it's written to a formula. Others say it's syrupy and flowery; abundant with adjective overload. In truth, good travel writing is neither and this genre is a bit more complicated than its two-word name indicates.

Types of travel articles

There is no such thing as a traditional travel article. While most define the destination piece as travel writing per se, travel stories come in a melange of shapes and sizes. Following are the various types of articles within this category.

Adventure

Usually involving a physical endeavour, many of these pieces cover soft adventure experiences like hiking, jeeping, white water rafting, snowmobiling, horseback riding. Keep in mind that successful adventure pieces can be authored by an expert, as well as a novice, because readers include first-timers, too.

Day trips

Sharing a little-known aspect of a well-travelled route is the purpose of the day trip story. These travel articles are typically spin-offs of better known destinations in the Lisbon or San Francisco category. Day trip pieces on these respective cities, for example, could be Sintra (summer residence of Portugal's kings) and Muir Woods (the Northern California home to giant redwood trees). Note that a critical element of the day trip story is found in the details – how far away it is, how to get there, days and hours of operation, costs, etc.

Destination

These travel pieces focus on the *place*, whether it's Hong Kong or Hawaii, California or China, Sydney or Singapore. But out-of-the-way haunts like Obidos and Oberstdorf have destination appeal too; perhaps more for some editors who are in constant quest of the new and little-heard-of spots.

First-person narrative

While some publications shy away from first-person accounts of a travel experience, many do not, if written properly. A first-person narrative is not the verbatim rendition of a travel diary; it is the creative compilation of colourful description, anecdotes, comparisons and contrasts from your personal perspective.

Food and drink

Because readers engage daily in these two activities, food and drink are timeless travel topics. You needn't be a chef de haute cuisine to write about gourmet dining, but you should learn the basics of cooking. A standard food and drink story might include history of the restaurant, the chef's background, an account of your dining experience, price ranges and recipes of signature dishes.

Holiday/historic/anniversary dates

Be aware that these types of travel articles require substantial lead time; this means approaching an editor months in advance. Holidays like Christmas or Valentine's Day, the anniversary of President John F. Kennedy's death or D-Day and the annual Melbourne Cup (Australia's most popular horse race that virtually halts the nation) are natural pegs for travel stories.

One example of tying a universally recognized date to a travel piece might be a story featuring the history of Wimbledon, coinciding with England's late June/early July Wimbledon Lawn Tennis Championships.

How-to/travel tips

Advice about subjects like women travelling safely, how to pack, bargaining in a Mexican bazaar and international travel with children is the core of these travel pieces. Often, the best lead for a how-to piece is an anecdote of a potential misadventure.

Humour

Typical travel situations are as fraught with frustration as they are with fun. Think about it. Pairing a first-time visit to an exotic destination with unfamiliar customs and a foreign language is the recipe for humour.

News slant

Sometimes there is interest in the travel piece about a place in a
state of flux. While readers would not opt to spend a holiday in
a potential war zone or dangerous destination, these spots are
nevertheless intriguing. Your ability to take the reader behind
the scenes might capture the interest of an editor. This is
especially true of an area recently reopened to tourists. Places
like Cuba and Vietnam fall into this category.

Roundup

This type of travel article covers between five and ten different
places with a common link. A spa roundup, for example, could
have a title like 'Southern California Day Spas', 'European-Style
Spas in South America' or 'Spas Specializing in Seaweed Wraps'.
The commonality in all these stories is the spa; the location is
secondary. In a roundup the lead paragraph introduces the
central theme, followed by the individually featured elements.

Special interest

Designed to inform travellers of a hobby, activity or manner of
travel one can pursue when away from home, the special
interest piece can cover an assortment of topics. Potential
subjects include antiquing, sports, shopping, eateries, lodging,
family travel, luxury travel or budget travel – anything of
particular interest to the reader that occurs in a specific locale.

Titles like 'Golf the Scottish Way in St Andrews', 'Washington
DC: A Family Affair', 'Staying in Portugal's *Pousadas*' or
'Travelling with a Pampered Pet' illustrate special interest travel
pieces.

Transit

Getting there is the story. Whether you ride a *burro* up the
mountain to local lodging, skim across the midnight waters by
hydrofoil to an exclusive island resort, train through India or
bike in Burgundy, the transportation experience is the core of
the piece. The destination becomes a less important story focus
than the romance and excitement of reaching it.

Ideas

'Where do you find ideas?' is a question I'm often asked. My standard response: 'Everywhere.' Even on airplanes.

Toward the beginning of my travel writing career I met Colin Dangaard, an Australian tour operator/horseman/entertainment personality on a flight between New York and Los Angeles. Attired in a cowboy hat and all the matching gear, he greeted me with a 'G'day' as he sat next to me. When his like-attired friend wished me 'G'luck', I buckled my seat belt, knowing I was in for a memorable ride.

I discovered that my seatmate was an insatiable entrepreneur, who lived in Malibu, CA, and his latest venture was a ten-day equestrian tour of North Queensland, his boyhood stomping grounds. The tour was a true family operation: brother John acted as camp supervisor, their sister Camelia handled the cleaning and laundry and Mum entertained the group in her home. The brochure read: 'Ride like the man from Snowy River.'

As a contributor to *Travel People*, a magazine featuring travel industry folks in out-of-the-norm roles, I recognized that I had uncovered a story idea shortly after sitting next to *it*. The resulting piece was entitled: 'Colin Dangaard: Malibu's Crocodile Dundee.'

In another airplane incident, I noticed my seatmate dealing with an oversized wooden container before takeoff. He, the flight attendant and even the captain were trying to find a place to store the piece.

'Where did you put your carry-on?' I asked once he sat down. When he replied the cockpit, my investigative instincts told me it was an important item. I wasn't disappointed. The gentleman next to me was the official escort of the America's Cup. The wooden container housed the prized trophy. I proceeded with an interview written on the airline's cocktail napkin.

Uncovering ideas is typically an unplanned exercise. I may have harvested a few while on an airplane; but they come in an assortment of settings. Inspiration can hit when I'm researching another story, overhearing a conversation at the coffee shop or in the grocery queue and see a tabloid headline.

Notice what's timely. Did a centuries-old hotel recently reopen? Spot trends. Do the latest buzz words MINKS (multiple income, no kids) and OINKS (one income, no kids) tickle your curiosity about their travel preferences?

Seek the superlative (the first, only, biggest, smallest, newest, most expensive, best value). Freelancer Chris Rodell authored a piece entitled 'Town Saved by Ball of Twine' about the universe's largest ball of twine collected by a single person. At 11 feet, 9 inches high and 40 feet around, the 8.7-ton tourist site is credited with breathing life into the tiny town (250 residents) of Darwin, Minnesota.

How did the freelancer uncover the twine idea? The curious journalist explained:

> *I was reading the* Star Tribune, *Minneapolis' newspaper, and it jumped out at me. Although I was in Minnesota to do another story, I drove 1½ hours out of my way to see it because it's a typical Americana roadside story.*

> *There are thousands of travel writers going to the Himalayas and thousands going to glamour spots. Editors get those stories all the time. So you have to look for the offbeat. During a trip to the Everglades I was wined and dined at Marco Island. But my best story idea didn't come from the beautiful surroundings and the gourmet food; it was a piece on a blind 75-year-old alligator wrestler.*

It was some tidbits found in the following readers' forum letter that sparked my interest in airline travel:

> *How many miles does one fly while eating a meal on a jet aircraft? This question bothered an Air France hostess on a recent flight, so she conducted a survey during the introduction of the [airline's] 575-mile-an-hour Boeings on the New York to Paris route. The results: one can have a glass of champagne and cover 150 miles; an hors d'oeuvre, 150 miles; appetizer, 100 miles; soup, 50 miles; entree and wine, 450 miles; dessert, 150 miles; cup of coffee, 100 miles; liqueur, 170 miles. This survey shows that passengers can eat and drink more than one-third of a 3175 nautical-mile trip.*

Even trivia can spawn an idea.

Research

Once the idea is determined, it's time to research. As we saw in Chapter 03, research can come from a variety of sources:

libraries, Internet, national tourist offices, convention and visitors' bureaus, chambers of commerce, public relations firms, personal files and on-the-road experiences.

Every writer deals with research in his own way. Here's how writer Katharine Dyson does it:

> I'm often asked how I organize my research for writing. On a research trip, I take notes only on those things not found in press kits. For example I might jot down a good quote or I might notice that what is described as a garden view is actually that of a parking lot. I arrive home after a press jaunt loaded with brochures, business cards and other materials.

Coupled with research unearthed from other sources, the writer is ready to write.

Query

Called the query, this letter is written to the editor and is the most important sales tool in a scribe's arsenal. While the query will be covered thoroughly in Chapter 08, the following description addresses the basics.

This letter of inquiry should clearly define the story idea, be tightly focused, tell why the story would be of interest to the publication's readers (this demonstrates you know their market) and show you're the writer to do it (mention where your work has appeared). The query is a one-page letter. It should be single spaced and have no typographical errors or misspellings (especially the editor's name).

Accompanied by published clips of your work, the query is designed to convince the editor you are the writer to do the job. Once completed, send the query, clips and an SAE to a selection of editors. While it's not the norm, include slide duplicates of especially good photography. Exceptional visuals may make the difference between a sale and a rejection.

Go-ahead

Inexperienced writers send out one or two queries and then wait. Veteran travel writers match an idea with several publications. They blanket these markets with queries; and they query one idea after another. But when any travel writer – beginner or veteran – gets the go-ahead, he should be ready to go.

A positive response can come in two forms. The most typical go-ahead missive for a new writer (beginner or new to the publication) is, 'Yes, on spec'. This reply means the editor likes your idea and agrees to accept your completed manuscript on speculation; he is making no commitment to buy the finished product.

The best reply, of course, is to receive a concrete assignment from the publication. Once magazine editors assign a piece, they often follow up with a letter confirming the terms of the agreement. (Newspapers rarely send assignment letters.)

Then there are some magazines that send contracts – longer, more detailed documents stipulating the terms. It is important to read carefully whatever document is sent. Be sure to contact the editor to clarify any questions or concerns you may have before signing and returning the official paper.

If no document is supplied, it's smart to recap the verbally discussed terms in a letter sent to the editor. Items to include are the article's working title; the agreed date of completion, the scheduled date of publication; the number of words; the deadline; the rights you are selling; the fee; payment schedule (paid on acceptance or paid on publication); photo terms, if applicable; whether this is an on-spec or confirmed assignment and information about a kill fee (should the article not run).

Negotiation

Negotiation may be as simple as an editor saying, 'We pay US $400 for a 2000 to 2200-word article'. This statement is straightforward and does not appear to invite arbitration. In these instances, however, I make a habit of asking, 'Is there room in your budget for a little more?' or 'Could you go as high as US $500 for the 2200-word piece?' If the request is made in a professional, non-threatening manner, the worst response is a 'no' and the best translates into more money.

In a real negotiation situation, however, it's important to be savvy. It's like a game of poker. Let me share a bargaining situation which netted successful results. A publication with which I was unaccustomed contacted me about writing a 2000-word advertorial and asked what I would charge.

I explained that because I wasn't familiar with the magazine I would not be able to give an immediate answer. But I requested a recent issue (illustrating an advertorial), along with details of their standard payment range. I, in turn, sent clips of my work; and we agreed to discuss the assignment once we had exchanged this information.

By express mail I received the publication – but no price list. My response was to call writer friends. 'What would they charge?' I asked. Their answers varied from US $1,000 to US $1/word (universally considered very good pay).

The editor called and although I was prepared, I wanted him to take the lead. He asked how much I would charge. 'Mel, I have no desire to be your highest paid contributor', I began. 'I want to be fair. So tell me what you normally pay and if it's not enough, we can negotiate'. Mel's response, 'US $3,500'. 'That's fair', I said.

But money is not the only negotiable component in a writer/publication arrangement. Other items an established travel writer might pursue are: travel expenses; telephone, mailing, faxing expenses and extended deadlines, if needed (editors almost always give artificial deadlines).

Story elements

Certain elements comprise any story. The place to start is the lead – the beginning. It could be the first sentence, first paragraph, the first several paragraphs. A lead is like following a directional signal. It says, 'The story is taking you this route'.

Transitions move the piece along, give it flow and smoothly connect paragraph to paragraph. They can be words like *meanwhile* and *after all* or transitional sentences similar to 'We finally reached the peak's summit'. The most effective transitions can be phrases that compare and contrast. After writing a paragraph about a rainy day in New York, for example, the next paragraph might start, 'Under sunny skies, New York ...'.

A good ending is almost as significant as a good beginning. Noted author Mickey Spillane says: 'Your first page sells your book, the last sells your next book.' The same principle applies to newspaper and magazine articles.

An article's conclusion is like adding a *full stop* or an *exclamation point* to the piece. Often it is a summation – it tells where you've been and what you learned. Good closings aren't written to a formula. An effective finish might be a tailor-made anecdote. Or it could tie the ending with the beginning, bringing the piece full circle. The best ending, however, is rarely a lengthy one.

The writing process

Inspiration is wonderful when it happens, but the writer must develop an approach for the rest of the time. The approach must involve getting something down on the page: something good, mediocre or even bad.

Leonard S. Bernstein

Now it's time to put the ingredients together; the process is similar to following a recipe. This step of the writing process – getting it on paper – is the most difficult. More than likely, every sentence written needs work. That is expected during this stage called *roughing it*. The object is to let the words flow and create a first draft. It's been said the standard ratio is 1:2; about half of what is written in the first draft is worthy enough to keep.

Katharine Dyson explains:

When I'm ready to write, I start with my notes (which could already be in my laptop: I often take it with me). I begin writing, letting the ideas free flow without regard as to whether or not they're in the right place or even if I eventually will use them.

As I write, I often organize the material by subheads, especially when the piece is long and complex. For example, subheads might include background, history, attractions, hotels, restaurants and transportation.

Once everything is entered, I start the editing process and work to get the introductory paragraph right. After I do this, the rest is fairly easy. There are times that little editing is needed; others when I surgically lop out a great chunk.

The first edit stage is when you separate the good from the bad. It is during this stage that you determine the precise verbiage, the best images and the most lyrical blend of words and meaning. This is the time to follow Mark Twain's ageless advice: 'Use the right word and not its second cousin'.

It is also at this stage that spelling and punctuation are corrected, as well as structural problems like run-on sentences and subject-verb agreement. Is the article written in the same person? Is it written in the same tense? Are there redundant statements? If time allows, set the piece aside for a week, then review it when you can approach it with more objectivity.

If there's no time, self edit the piece now. And whether now or later, read the piece several times, always aloud, during the first edit. The ear can pick up what the eye alone cannot – it can hear awkward verbiage.

The second edit is when you'll reach beyond the norm and delve into your imagination. Fine tune your manuscript. Will two words suffice for the five you used? Avert adjective overload. Avoid words like *really* and *very* (overusing these modifiers weakens rather than intensifies your meaning). This is the time to shape, hone and mould.

The time to *perfect* is in the final draft, a no-typo, error-free manuscript – the last step of the writing process.

> *[Mistakes] reveal that you have not paid attention to your own writing and invite the reader to respond in kind.*
>
> Richard A. Lanham

Manuscript format

There are no hard-and-fast rules about how a manuscript must look. When submitting a manuscript for possible publication, however, you can increase your chances of a sell by making a favourable and professional impression with its physical format.

The upper left corner of a manuscript's front page should list (single space) your formal name (rather than your pen name), address, phone number, e-mail address (if applicable) and social security number. Note that pseudonyms or pen names are a matter of personal preference. I personally like to see my own name in print but I have used a pseudonym when writing for competitive magazines.

The rights (example: First North American Serial) you are offering and the approximate word count of the manuscript are indicated in the upper right corner. (This information should be single spaced.) On the second and following pages type your name, a shortened version of the title and the page number e.g. Dial/Spas/Pg. 1 of 8. (This identification is called the *slug*.)

Most computers can provide you with a word count. But in the event that you must manually determine the number of words in your manuscript, use the following formula: add the number of characters and spaces in an average line and divide by six for the average words per line; multiply this number by the number of lines of type on a representative page to find the average number of words per page; multiply this number (average number of words per page) by the number of manuscript pages.

The word count should be approximate. Depending on the article's length, round off to the nearest 100 or 1000; round to the nearest 50 if the article is under 1000 words.

If requested, include an author's identification line at the end of the story, for instance: 'Sandra Anderson is a freelance writer who specializes in travel articles and lives in Dallas, Texas.'

Type and double space the text on white 20-pound bond paper. Margins should be 1 to 1½ inches on all sides of the manuscript. Do not justify the right margin because it can throw off the word count. Centre the title in capital letters about one-third of the way down the first page. Use standard paragraph indentations of five spaces. Select an easily readable font; font size should be 12 point. At the end of the manuscript write 'End'. And do not staple pages together; use a paper clip.

Manuscript package

Submission of your completed manuscript is in a package format. This package will include a letter-perfect manuscript (always keep a copy for your files), requested photographs with a caption sheet (detailed in Chapter 12), an SAE (for return of photographs), an invoice (see example on next page) and a cover letter.

A cover letter should be brief – stating the package inclusions – and include customary pleasantries. While this is not a query and you needn't sell the piece again, some writers enclose a copy of the go-ahead or assignment letter to ensure recognition of a requested manuscript.

Many of today's publications request electronic submission of your manuscript or for you to provide it on disk. In either event, you should also provide a hard copy of your completed work. Photos and an invoice would also be included in this package.

Sample Invoice

Cynthia W. Dial
(Address) ● San Diego, CA 92130 USA
(Phone #) ● (Fax #)
E-mail cynthiadial1@aol.com
Invoice

To: Name of publication   Invoice No: 6050
    Address   Invoice Date: 11/12/02

Attn: Name of contact   (Social Security Number)

_____

                                            Description Amount
'Seeing New York'   (MAR)   US $400.00

Please pay this amount: US $400.00

_____

Please remit to: Cynthia Dial
                   Address
                   San Diego, CA 92130 USA

(*Note to the newcomer*: Don't use 1 as the number of your first issued invoice. It says *beginner*. Rather, start with a number like 1001.)

SAE (SASE) advice

One tip regarding the self-addressed stamped envelope is to send a letter size envelope – not one large enough for the return of your manuscript and clips. Avoid tempting the editor. Don't make it easier for him to return your manuscript than to return a note saying 'Go ahead'. One exception to this rule regards photography; always include an envelope and postage to accommodate the return of pictures.

Acceptance

Coupled with an editor's acceptance of a manuscript is his input. What exactly can you anticipate from an editor during this stage of the writing game? Don't expect an editor to polish tiresome material. It's not his job. No editor will pull out a thesaurus to make your work publishable.

However, the following advice is given to save a lot of heartache: the name *editor* means they edit. It is their job. They may rearrange paragraphs, make cuts or even change the title; sometimes without consulting the writer. This is not the stage to argue with the editor. Accept the changes. And if rewrites are requested, happily do them.

Payment and publication

Depending on the terms of payment – payment on acceptance (POA) or payment on publication (POP) – a cheque will arrive accordingly. Because lead times can be as long as nine to 12 months, the obvious preferred payment designation is POA as opposed to POP. (Note that most newspapers pay only after the article appears.)

There are other factors to consider, too. I have worked with several advertising-driven publications where, for example, an article on Asia assigned for the December issue might not run until sufficient media space is sold to Asian advertisers. Many times the articles never run. But I always get paid – I work on a POA basis.

With a POP arrangement, I would receive a kill fee if the assigned piece were not used. This fee is approximately half of the negotiated price for a published piece. For this reason, it's important to understand the kill fee policy before signing a contract or a letter of agreement.

The final step of the publication-of-an-article process is one that is many times neglected – thank you notes. Make copies of the article and send them with a note to especially helpful sources, for example interview subjects, individual hotels or restaurants, airline carrier(s), national tourist office(s), public relations firm, whomever made the article a reality.

08
the all-important query

In this chapter you will learn:
- the definition of a query
- query components
- how to query through examples.

The definition of a query is just as it sounds – a letter of inquiry. The end result of this *letter to the editor* is a definitive yes or no to your proposed story idea. A query can result in a sell before the story's written. Sometimes editor feedback may transform a good idea into a great story; at other times, it may discourage a piece entirely.

To a novice, a query may represent an added step to the writing procedure. But to the veteran it's a step saver. In truth, it's the most direct route to seeing your name in print.

Saves time/saves money

Sent in lieu of an unsolicited manuscript, a query saves time, conserves energy and is cost efficient. It eliminates spending hours writing an article that may not sell. And it is less expensive to send ten one-page query letters than an equal number of eight-page manuscripts.

If a query generates a positive response, the editor is likely to guide you to meet his specific needs, whether they be a 1000- versus a 2500-word piece or a first-person narrative as opposed to a third-person account. Some editors may even make a suggestion with respect to the article's focus. It's understandable that most editors like to have input; because after giving you the affirmative nod, it's in their best interest that you write a successful piece.

But if you get the go-ahead with no further specifications, the editor assumes you know his publication's needs regarding the size and style of its articles.

Editor etiquette

Personalize your letter as much as possible. Direct the correspondence to the correct editor – it may be the travel editor, the managing editor or the features editor. And in the case of a small- to middle-sized publication where it's not clear from the masthead, query the top person.

Once you've determined the best editor to approach, get the name right and use it. If in doubt, proceed as previously suggested: invest in a telephone call or e-mail an inquiry to confirm the spelling and gender. And don't try to establish a bond by addressing the editor by his first name in the salutation (that is, unless you are personally acquainted or have previously worked with that editor).

Respect the editor's time. Be brief and to the point. Stick to the one-page rule. I recall one editor's notation in her correspondence: 'Please excuse the form letter. To expedite the return of the 100 or more stories we receive some weeks, such is necessary. I have no secretary and often have to read freelance after hours and on weekends. Thanks for understanding.'

Query lead as story lead

The query should be designed to grab an editor's interest about your irresistible topic. Your beginning is the single most important component of this letter of persuasion. Its opening paragraph should be as captivating and invoke as much interest as the lead of the travel article itself.

Many times this opening paragraph, if as good as it should be, becomes your manuscript's lead. Composing a winning lead has a dual benefit. It is used initially to solicit the editor's interest; and once accomplished, the same lead can become the story introduction.

Other necessary components

The five Ws: who, what, when, where, why (how) usually follow the lead. This is where you succinctly summarize your proposed story idea. Tell the editor why your idea fits his readership; this shows you've done your homework and are familiar with the publication.

Write the query to reflect the tone of your intended piece. For a humour piece, write in light and lively language. Whereas a Veteran's Day piece on Arlington National Cemetery would be expressed in a more sombre vein. And if you have a catchy title, it will help sell the piece. Words in the title like *new, free* and *best* get attention; so do how-to articles with names such as 'Six Ways to Save Money in Paris'.

If you have publishing credits, mention them. Share the interviews you plan to include in the piece. List your sources, particularly if you have distinctive personalities lined up. If you are proposing a piece on Sedona, Arizona's Enchantment Resort and the concierge is the nation's only Native American in that capacity, tell the editor.

Perhaps you have special skills or in-depth personal experience in an area or with a destination. Who better to write a story about Northern Ireland than you, for example, if you spent two years in Belfast.

Include the nuts and bolts of the proposed article: working title (if available), a suggested format, projected due date, availability and type of photography. You can also include the manuscript length; but first research the publication to determine the number of words in a typical article.

Salespeople are routinely taught to ask for the sale. As a writer, don't make the mistake of assuming the editor knows what you want. The verbiage is insignificant. It can be as simple as: 'This story has the potential to inspire readers to pack their bags and head to Rio. I'd love to write it for *Aboard*.' But whatever method you choose, close the deal.

Think about the value of the PS, the *postscript*. It's guaranteed to be read so use it wisely. If you're pitching a piece 'Dine Where the *Celebs* Do', a PS with a note like 'Steve Martin is a meat-and-potatoes kind of guy. He and Martin Short sat at a table next to ours at the Polo Lounge' is certain to get most editors' attention.

Do not neglect to date the letter. And don't forget to include contact information (not provided on the letterhead) in the query: street address, phone number, fax, e-mail address.

Extras

It is appropriate for the query package to have additional inclusions. One addendum is a one- to two-paragraph bio. Keep in mind a bio is not a fully fledged CV; it's a brief synopsis of your journalistic background.

A bio includes writing credits, followed by information like writing-related positions (e.g. editor of *ABC Travel Magazine*, writing instructor at *XYZ University*), educational background and memberships in professional organizations. Additional personal information should be included only if it's relevant and will help sell your piece.

Some writers prefer sending a pre-printed self-addressed stamped postcard (SAP) opposed to the SAE, because it expedites the reply process, plus it's cheaper (see the following example). While it certainly creates an effortless response, it may inadvertently encourage a *no* because it may be easier to put a tick in a box than to put a letter in an envelope.

SAP sample for query

Dear editor: Thank you for your consideration re: <u>('name of article' filled in by writer)</u>. To conserve your limited time, please tick the appropriate space(s).

___ Yes, I am interested. Send the article.

___ Colour slides   ___ B&W prints   ___ No photos

___ I can't use the article now but would like to consider it for future use.

___ Can't use this subject because _____

Other comment _____

Editor's name _____ Date _____

Publication <u>(filled in by writer)</u> _____

Query analysis

Following is a query letter which resulted in interest from three non-competing newspaper editors.

Sample query – 'Israel – a safe trip'

Dear (name of editor):

December 9 was the one-year anniversary of the *Intifada* – the Arab uprising in Jerusalem. This year Christmas celebrations were cancelled in Bethlehem because without peace, officials felt there was nothing to celebrate. Yasir Arafat was denied a US visa at the beginning of December. Only the United States and Israel backed the decision.

I left the United States for Israel on December 5, was in Jerusalem by December 9 and in Bethlehem on December 10. It was not without trepidation that, as a first-time visitor, I went to Israel.

However, I also visited the Western Wall on the last day of Hanukkah, sang Christmas carols in Bethlehem's Church of the Nativity and swam leisurely in the Dead Sea. Apart from reading about the *tense* situation in *USA TODAY* each morning on the bus, my travelling companions and I were unaware of any problems and were never concerned for our safety.

As one travel editor said: 'More and more we have to deal with travel in a volatile world, finding those destinations where readers can feel at ease, not on guard.' If planned properly, Israel *is* one of those destinations. After the bombing of Pan Am's Flight 103, Israel via El Al seems an even more viable destination as the airline's security procedures are unrivalled.

May I share my piece entitled 'Israel – A Safe Trip' with your readers? The story can be illustrated with my 35mm colour slides or B&W prints and can be delivered two weeks after your go-ahead.

I'm including sample clips to demonstrate my usual style and approach. It is not necessary to return the clips, only your comments in the enclosed SAE. Thank you for your consideration. I look forward to hearing from you.

Sincerely,

Cynthia Dial

Let's dissect it. The opening paragraphs took the better part of a morning to write but it was not wasted time; they were used as the resulting article's lead. A high-profile current event – Israel's potentially volatile situation – was used to grab the editors' interest.

Specific dates detailed in the second paragraph underscored my proximity to the action. These sentences basically say, *I was in the thick of it.* (This doesn't mean, however, that the recitation of a personal diary would be of interest to any editor.)

The purpose of the third paragraph was to contradict what one might expect in a latent war zone. The statement 'reading *USA TODAY* each morning on the bus' was incorporated to connect the editor with the harmless reality of the situation.

The quote that began 'More and more. . .' was from the editor of *Travel & Leisure* magazine; it was found in *Writer's Market*. This editor's words were used to add validity to the article's premise that people need to know Israel is safe. Pan Am's Flight

103 was cited because of the Lockerbie, Scotland, incident, which had occurred recently.

The final paragraph asked for the sale. It also included the nuts and bolts of the piece. I purposely excluded the expected word count because the query was submitted to multiple newspapers with differing needs.

Another sample query follows.

Sample query – San Diego theatre

Dear (name of editor):

When packing for a visit to the fun-in-the-sun capital of San Diego, one does not forget a swimsuit, the camera for a photo opportunity at the city's world-famous zoo or even a surfboard; but opera glasses are usually set aside to make room for suntan lotion.

The undeniable truth is that in addition to serving up the nation's most perfect weather, San Diego also offers a variety of close to 100 performing arts groups whose reputations attract nationally and internationally recognized talent, giving travellers additional reasons to return to California's second largest city again and again.

'The best thing about San Diego is we've got it all – the surf, the sun, the zoo, Shamu … but when the sun goes down, the curtain comes up', states San Diego Theater League's executive director Alan Ziter. Broadway hits such as 'Big River', 'Into the Woods' and 'The Who's Tommy' originated at La Jolla Playhouse, winner of the recent Tony Award for outstanding regional theatre. Playwright Neil Simon even previewed and tested his play, 'The Cocktail Hour', on local audiences at the Old Globe Theatre (another Tony Award winner) before its New York debut.

The *San Francisco Chronicle* said: 'San Diego is now arguably the most important point of origin in the country for regional theater productions aimed at Broadway and off-Broadway and a commercial future beyond'. But while theater critics and a small minority are aware of San Diego's reputation in the thespian world, most are not.

May I share with your readers this secret that California's southernmost city has, until now, kept under its beach blanket? The article will run from 2000 to 2500 words and can be delivered about three weeks after receiving a go-ahead. If interested, I can provide photography to illustrate the piece.

To acquaint you with my writing, I am enclosing clips of my work. It is not necessary to return the clips, only your comments in the enclosed SASE (SAE). I look forward to hearing from you.

Sincerely,

Cynthia Dial

Use quotes, statistics, anecdotes

Quotes create a sense of authority. They bring a piece to life, many times allowing you to make a point that might be awkward if expressed in the third person. They give your manuscript colour.

I toured Egypt after the occurrence of a number of *incidents* (government lingo for terrorist activities linked to Middle Eastern extremists). Tourism was at a complete standstill; a nine-word quote summarized the situation. My piece read: 'A darkly-robed elderly attendant, whose job was to collect shoes of those entering Cairo's Mosque of Mohammed Ali, commented in Arabic to my tour guide. She translated, 'A mosque without tourists is like food without salt'.

Citing relevant facts and statistics builds a solid foundation for a story idea. Including these specifics is a good way to convince the editor you're qualified to write the piece. The following fact-inspired lead was used in a query which resulted in a front-page travel section article in *The Denver Post*:

> *Over 32 million people visited San Diego last year. Of that number, 23% crossed the border into Tijuana. However, few of these day visitors knew enough about the area to venture beyond this Mexican town.*

The anecdotal lead is a perennial favourite. The definition of an anecdote is a short account of an incident or event of an interesting or amusing nature. The aim of this lead style is to immediately involve the reader and then tell the story behind the story. History of the famed America's Cup inspired this lead:

> *In 1851 an American schooner,* America, *raced against a fleet of 15 British schooners around the Isle of Wight.* America *finished the course so far ahead of the others that*

the schooner's showing inspired the legendary exchange between Queen Victoria and one of her attendants. 'Who is first?' the queen asked when the lone boat appeared upon the horizon. When told it was America, *she asked who was placed second. 'Your Majesty', came the reply, 'there is no second'.*

Query research

Your research objective should be to uncover just enough information to compose an authoritative query; not to write the entire piece. But be certain to do sufficient research to convince the editor you know your subject. You must include enough facts in the query to instil a feeling of confidence. Writers walk a fine line between taking shortcuts in the research process and endlessly researching a topic to the exclusion of ever getting around to writing the piece. Find a happy medium.

Research doesn't have to be a laborious task; often you can get enough facts with a phone call or two. Use your reference librarian to answer certain questions: 'How many islands comprise the Bahamas archipelago?' or 'What is today's Australian foreign exchange rate compared to that of ten years ago?'

Your telephone directory is an underestimated resource. Need some information on travelling with a dog? Call one or two local veterinarians. Want to compare the cost of a flight to Rome with one to Milan? Telephone an international airline.

If you're having trouble finding experts, consult a library reference called *The Encyclopedia of Associations*. This resource contains names of organizations that can provide facts by phone and later mail brochures, booklets, reprints of previous articles on your topic, even books, at no cost.

And of course, one of the most popular research sources at the moment is the library sitting on your desktop – the Internet. One word of caution: don't make the assumption that because information is found on the Internet, it is up to date. You may want to double-check questionable facts by cross-referencing them to another source. Generally speaking, however, material provided by governmental organizations, major companies and notable non-profit associations is valid and accurate.

One idea versus several

It's probably best for the beginner to query one story idea at a time; not to offer three or four ideas with a one-paragraph description of each. Why? It's too difficult for a novice to sell a full article by saying so little (a paragraph isn't enough space to showcase your ability).

But once you get established and have a collection of clips, you may want to consider shopping several story ideas at a time. The following samples illustrate a couple of different approaches.

Sample multi-idea query 1

Dear (name of editor):

I am spending next winter in Williamsburg, Virginia. While there, I would be happy to research a story for *Historic Traveller*. Would any of the following topics appeal to your readers?

- Duke of Gloucester Street (historic lane lined with restored homes depicting Colonial Williamsburg during the 1700s).
- The beginnings of the College of William and Mary (the city's renowned university and the nation's oldest).
- An insider's tour of Williamsburg's colonial craft shops, like the Blacksmith Shop (where a master blacksmith works at an anvil while his helper fans a fire in the forge).

[The above story ideas are each followed by a two to three-sentence description designed to grab the editor's interest.]

Sample multi-idea query 2

Dear (name of editor):

As a regular reader of *Endless Vacation*, I always enjoy your focus on luxury travel. And as a veteran traveller, my eternal quest is to stay at the best. Can I interest you in a piece on any one of the following recently-visited properties that specialize in pampering?

- Four Seasons Nevis (the Caribbean's only five-star resort).
- Beverly Hills Hotel (Hollywood's haunt).
- Dorchester Hotel (one of London's finest).

[Each of the listed topics is followed by a two to three-sentence tightly-focused, highly-crafted description.]

Once a working relationship is developed, some travel writers have been successful in receiving additional assignments by providing the editor with a list of recently-visited destinations. This tactic is not suggested for a new writer; it should be reserved for an already established writer/editor kinship.

Grab the editor's attention

Avoid using clever tactics to set your query apart from its competitors. This means no pink stationery and no cutesy verbiage. One of the best ways to get an editor's attention, however, is to include published clips. Let's face it, editors are human. And most are simply more comfortable working with a writer others have recognized as *good enough to publish*.

Select your clips carefully if you have a bevy from which to choose. Consider including recent ones (indicating you are an active travel writer). Clips from high-profile publications are always impressive. And one or two clips relevant to the topic you are pitching are a tremendous bonus. Whatever you submit, submit samples of your best.

If this is a query for a reslanted article, don't make the mistake of sending a clip of the originally published piece to acquaint the editor with your work. And if you have no clips in your portfolio, don't despair. Read on.

Treat like a CV

A query is like a CV. It should accentuate the positives and ignore the negatives. If you have no clips, don't feel obliged to announce this fact. Skip the explanation: 'As a relatively new writer, I am not sending clips because I am not yet published.'

Simply compose a cohesive, impeccably crafted query – showcasing your ability to write well. Nothing sells a story idea better than good, solid writing.

Present yourself professionally. Use a letterhead denoting you as a travel writer, travel journalist, writer/photographer, whatever title you select. It makes you look and feel professional. And submit a letter-perfect query – this means no typos, no misspellings, no grammatical errors.

To query or not to query

As discussed in Chapter 05, it's not necessary to query the newspaper market. However, I always do (see 'Israel – a safe trip' sample on page 101). A quick query enables me to organize my story idea and assess the market's interest. As a businesswoman I have no desire to invest a week (even a couple of days) on a piece that, for one reason or another, is simply not right.

Other exceptions to the *query rule* include articles that translate poorly in a query format, such as a humour piece or short filler. The general rule of thumb is to send the article itself for a piece with fewer than 1000 words. And it goes without saying that a manuscript should be sent when specifically instructed by the publication to do so. (Writers guidelines and reference books like *Writer's Market* indicate these preferences.) To do otherwise might result in the return of a query with no response.

Telephone pitch dilemma

An editor's time is limited. Thus, the best approach (especially for the beginning journalist) is not to call but to query an editor. Once you're established and have worked regularly with several editors, it will be possible to pick up the telephone and get an assortment of assignments without mailing one query. But for the meantime, stick to this informal rule: query, don't phone.

Of course, there are always exceptions to every rule. One exception to the query versus telephone rule is when your topic is time sensitive. If the time element is so limited that a delay would jeopardize the sale, send the manuscript itself or phone.

Freelancer Pamela Stone offers some tips to writers who telephone editors:

> Remember to write the idea down first. Have someone read it. Then, read it out loud and rehearse it over a tape recorder. You must have it down to a 30-second pitch. No more!

Bear in mind that a positive response generally takes longer than a *no*. But if it's been several months and you still haven't heard from an editor, does this constitute an exception to the telephone rule? For some travel writers, it does. However, I prefer a brief note of reminder, accompanied by an SASE (SAE) and a checklist. While it needs modification, this note can be patterned from the correspondence illustrated in the example given on page 148.

Query dos and don'ts

Do . . .

- Submit to the top. Don't shy away from prestigious, high-paying publications.
- Send query letters to a number of publishers at the same time.
- Have a positive frame of mind in the query-writing process.
- Use confident, assertive verbiage. (Don't say: 'I could share with your readers', say: 'I will tell your readers.')
- Enclose a business card.
- Include an SAE with correct return postage or IRCs (International Reply Coupons) for an out-of-country publication.
- Keep a copy of your query.
- Match the correct query letter with the correct envelope for multiple submissions.
- Track query submissions.

Don't . . .

- Oversell the piece. (Never promise something you cannot deliver.)
- Undersell yourself.
- Use vague references and foggy statistics. (Avoid weak proclamations such as, 'Monaco is comprised of an assortment of ethnic groups'. Instead say, 'Monaco's population is comprised of 47% French, 16% Italian and 16% Monegasque'.
- Vaguely describe rather than completely detail your story idea for fear an editor will steal your concept.
- Excessively use exclamation points. (Rather than conveying excitement to an editor, this punctuation mark actually dilutes the message.)
- Fax or e-mail a query unless it is at the editor's request.

09 elements of a good article

In this chapter you will learn:
- how to paint a travel picture
- the truth about titles
- the importance of objectivity
- interview techniques.

Certainly the object of travel writing is to impart the who, what, when, where, why and how of a destination. But its dual function is to share the five Ws of the journey in a creative, helpful, intriguing manner. Sounds easy, doesn't it? That's what many of my students believe – until they begin to write.

In truth, the equation for a good article is loaded with multiple variables. While not all travel pieces include the same components, the absence or sloppy development of a single element can sabotage an otherwise saleable piece. Thus, it makes sense to understand these basic fundamentals.

Begin at the beginning?

Your narrative will take the reader on a journey from lead to ending, but the sequence of the piece doesn't necessarily start at your trip's beginning. The order depends on the importance of your on-the-road episodes, not on the chronological succession of these events.

Start at the climactic moment – whatever point pulls the reader into the setting. It might be when the penguin brushed against your leg during a swim off the Galapagos' island of Bartholome. Perhaps it's the instant you reached into your coat pocket and realized your wallet had been lifted. Or it could be as serene a moment as emerging from the light-deprived military bunker atop Diamond Head to encounter the first rays of daybreak.

Close your eyes and take yourself back to the moment. Did you flinch at the initial feel of an unknown furry creature hidden in the water? Was the ocean warmed by the equatorial sun or was there a slight chill to it? What was the highlight of the experience? Relive that moment. Now put it on paper. It will transport you back to the locale faster than any jet airliner and transform your readers into passengers on that voyage.

Remember that as a travel writer you have the licence to distort time for effect, to develop or expand an on-location event for intrigue and to skip over the dullness. A travel piece is not a dissertation; it is not the appropriate writing forum for an hour-by-hour, day-by-day description of your journey.

... The best way to be boring is to leave nothing out.

Voltaire

Lead logic

It's difficult to exaggerate the significance of the lead. Thus, in quest of the best beginning, it's smart to explore every avenue in an exercise to uncover the uncommon. Listed here are some resources that aid the travel writer in this endeavour.

Quotation lead

Books like *Bartlett's Familiar Quotations* and *Simpson's Contemporary Quotations* can claim responsibility for innumerable travel story leads. I frequently use both sources.

But many of the primers I rely on were unearthed at flea markets or discovered in the back rooms of secondhand bookstores. These obscure treasures are loaded with leads. Ponder the rich possibilities of opening a piece with any of the following quotations:

> *The coldest winter I ever spent was a summer in San Francisco.*
>
> Mark Twain

> *When I went to Venice, my dream became my address.*
> Marcel Proust, in a letter to Madame Strauss

> *You cannot simply bring together a country that has 265 kinds of cheese.*
>
> Charles de Gaulle, on France

> *When it's three o'clock in New York, it's still 1938 in London.*
>
> Bette Midler

Anecdote lead

A colourful anecdote can transform a potentially dull subject into one of interest. Consider the following anecdotal lead incorporated into an assigned piece for a corporate and incentive travel trade magazine. The audience of the piece is the meeting planner and the subject is budgeting. (The source is *The Little Brown Book of Anecdotes*.)

> *Making meeting budgets stretch can be a real challenge when the bottom line is to produce a meeting that will in turn produce results. It is not a time for indiscriminate spending or for random budgeting as every dollar counts*

and must be well spent. In other words, this is not the time to recreate a George Raft scenario.

Film actor George Raft acquired and disposed of about [US] $10 million in the course of his career. The actor's explanation: 'Part of the loot went for gambling, part for horses and part for women. The rest I spent foolishly.'

Commonality lead

The resource book, *The Timetables of History*, is a great aid to the writer creating a commonality lead. It produces a year-by-year timeline (4500 BCE to the present day) by category: history/politics, literature/theatre, religion/philosophy/learning, visual arts, music, science/technology/growth and daily life.

This lead was constructed from information culled from the *Timetables* reference.

What do Van Gogh's 'The Yellow Chair,' the Kodak box camera and Tchaikovsky's Symphony No. 5 have in common? They debuted in 1888, the year California's historic Hotel del Coronado first opened its doors.

Show, don't tell

A travel writer is only as good as his ability to *paint a picture*. Let's face it, a travel essay is a painting whose brush is the typewriter (or a word processor these days).

What was the aroma of the Kona coffee? How did the weathered wrought iron gate feel beneath your hand? Were the giant redwoods just 'tall' or did they 'pierce through the roof of the sky'? What about the Flamenco dancer's colourful skirt? Did it simply 'revolve around her' or did it 'twirl about her like a kaleidoscopic carousel'?

Simile and metaphor are essential travel writing tools to the author in his quest to create a living, breathing piece. In Arizona, for example: 'Sunrise on the northern rim of the Grand Canyon was like a Polaroid shot developing before one's eyes.' And a Los Angeles freeway observed from an airplane after dark becomes 'a farm of red and white ants scurrying from one spot to another'.

'I rewrote the ending of A Farewell to Arms *thirty-nine times before I was satisfied', Ernest Hemingway once told*

an interviewer. 'Was there a problem there?' the interviewer wanted to know. 'What was it that stumped you?' 'Getting the words right', said Hemingway.

Judith Appelbaum

Use the word *yearn* instead of *long*. Replace *dug in* with *entrenched*. *Walk* becomes a *swagger*. Strive to find the exact word, not just the right word. Don't simply recount what a locale is like, use action verbs to reveal what it's like.

Armchair travellers want you to take them to the place. Action verbs like *unleash* and *ache* breathe oxygen into your work; reserve adjectives like *astonishing, beautiful* and *spectacular* for brochure copy.

Create creative non-fiction

Creative non-fiction has been described 'where journalism and storytelling meet'. A travel writer is both a journalist – bound by facts, opinions, observations, and other collected information – and an author dedicated to telling a persuasive story in a creative way.

Write like the masters do. Notice how Pulitzer Prize-winners Bob Woodward and Carl Bernstein bring the Watergate scandal to life in *All the President's Men*. Read non-fiction books like *The Executioner's Song* (Norman Mailer), *All Creatures Great and Small* (James Herriot) and *Travels With Charlie* (John Steinbeck). Study their succulent descriptions.

Then implement this knowledge culled from your studious endeavours and use concrete details and sensory imagery to describe your non-fiction scenes (for example: a raspy voice betrayed her two-pack-a-day habit; her elderly eyes wrinkled like used wrapping paper).

Write for the readers

Write for a well-defined audience. Identify it, envision it, get to know it. Then write to an individual in this audience – not their neighbour or their coworker, but to this one particular person. I like to envision my reader. I put a face on him (or her) and then I tell the story, just as I would to my best friend. Many times the 'oh, I forgot to tell you' part makes a great sidebar.

Readers wants facts. Fill the article with facts (checked and double-checked); but avoid recounting details that even your best friend isn't interested in hearing. Boring writing is as tiresome as a dull conversation.

How do you spot boring prose? The sentences resemble one another and sound alike. The writing style is common. The pace and sound are monotonic. The piece is fraught with repetition. The verbiage is tired. And worst of all, the reader stops before the end.

> *My most important piece of advice to all you would-be writers: when you write, try to leave out all the parts readers skip.*
>
> Elmore Leonard

Readability should be the first, not the last criterion for a travel article. But now the question 'What makes it readable?' must be answered. Proper grammar and punctuation help, but are only guidelines. Follow this standard: think of the reader at every step of the writing game. In the end, if the story is clear and answers a reader's questions or fulfils a need – it'll receive a top grade from your audience.

Vary the cadence

Develop a feel for the tempo of your writing. Listen for it. It's like matching lyrics to a musical piece's melody. Keep the readers moving forward so they won't lose interest, but slow the pace when you think they need time to digest the words or the surroundings of where you've taken them.

You can achieve this effect by weaving hard facts and direct quotes with colourful observation and delectible description. Vary sentence length. Use short, to-the-point missives mixed with flowing prose.

Eight ways to give your writing punch

- use short words
- use dense words
- use familiar words
- use foreign words for spice
- use active verbs
- use strong verbs
- use specific nouns
- use adjectives sparingly

Explore the unusual about the usual

Expand beyond the expected. Have you considered penning an Italian food and drink piece after your visit to Rome, for example? It's been done again and again. What about pitching an Israeli bar mitzvah article? Ditto. But an Italian bar mitzvah might get the attention of one of two editors.

When you're interested in deviating from the norm, it helps to mix and match items from a variety of common categories. Combining *unlike* subjects from the following list of five topics gives a peek at this virtually endless and effortless means to ferret out the uncommon.

Country: Italy, Vietnam, Mexico, France, Thailand, Israel, Netherlands, Australia.

Time of year: January, February, March, April, May, June, July, August, September, October, November, December.

Holiday: Easter, Chinese New Year, Christmas, Chanukah, Boxing Day.

Celebration: Wedding, baby christening, bar/bat mitzvah, funeral procession/wake, birthday.

Activities: Downhill skiing, picnicking, snorkelling, shopping, food marketing, sunbathing, singing, attending church.

Consider these combinations: celebrating Christmas during Australia's summer, experiencing Chinese New Year in Holland, finding a Roman Catholic church service in Cairo. Are you following? And the only ingredient necessary in this exercise is your imagination.

Don't break promises

It's possible to experience Paris' George V for $100 a day.

Is this is a good lead? Because this pricey Paris hotel is one of the world's most exclusive, the lead would certainly get the attention of many editors. But if the statement is followed by the qualifier, 'Of course, *experience* doesn't mean staying there', the lead becomes a trick. Dishonest attempts to capture interest in your tale anger both editors and readers.

Follow through on promises made in the lead. Anyone can write a lead that will attract attention; but if your initial statement isn't supported by what follows, it becomes an accomplice in the creation of a weak story.

The best way to avoid disappointing readers is to develop a mission statement, create a lead in accompaniment with a promise and maintain constant focus toward that end. I know some journalists who write the mission statement on a Post-It note and affix it above their desks as a continual reminder of the final goal.

Capture the *foreignness* of a place

One of the most effective means of revealing the essence of a place is to use foreign words in the text. The incorporation of greetings like *ciao* or *aloha,* food and drink references such as *souvlaki* or *vino blanco* or descriptive terms like *haute Bohème* is like adding saffron to enhance the flavour of a dish.

A sprinkling (not an abundance) of foreign words and expressions helps transport readers to a distant land. The mention of *goombah* says Caribbean, as surely as *ikebana* and *teppan-yaki* invoke an instant image of Japan.

Note the sound of sirens in Lyon, a pedicab's bicycle bell in Hong Kong and the incessant honking of cab horns in New York City. Intersperse a country's currency, whether it's the Malaysian ringgit, Mexican peso or Norwegian krone, and you've created a piece with a foreign flair.

Title tips

Consider the title part of the lead. Like saying *hello* when you answer the telephone, the title's your initial greeting to the article. It tells you where the story will take you (for instance a humorous title promises an amusing piece). One rule of thumb is that while an ordinary title won't halt a sale, an extraordinary one may transfer your piece from the *no* to the *yes* stack.

Some title information:

1 Think of a title as a newspaper headline or a movie marquee.
2 Good titles are short (usually no more than six words).
3 The title should reflect the slant and tone of the piece.
4 Reveal information in the title, don't hide it.

5 Name your piece after it's written (by starting with the title you create boundaries).

6 Test the title – say it aloud.

7 Be creative with titles but frugal with time (while a clever title can help sell a piece, an editor may change the title).

8 Remember that many (readers and editors alike) read *only* the title to determine whether to read a piece.

9 Re-title and resubmit difficult-to-sell articles.

Title types range from rhyming, alliterative and question titles to how-to, action-oriented, play-on-words and list titles. When writing this chapter and browsing through several publications, I discovered the following names for pieces: 'A Bunch of Bula' (subtitled: warnings about danger in Fiji don't ring true) and 'San Pedro's Port Whine' (complaints about a California port of call.) Do they work? They got *my* attention; but you're the judge.

The interview

Quotes, whether live or secondhand, humanize a written piece. Travel articles expectedly include concrete facts, coupled with beckoning descriptions. But it's the addition of information from authorities that helps convince readers that your theme is valid. And these personal interviews are a welcome departure from the world of adjectives otherwise necessary to create a picture in words.

Interview info

1 Select interviewees carefully. Don't interview someone just because he agrees to speak to you; interview if the person's input will add to the piece. That said, don't overlook an interview, even an informal one, that may provide the liveliest exchange and insight into a place, e.g. maitre d', theatre usher, etc.

2 Pre-interview advice includes: making a list of questions, calling to reconfirm the appointment, double-checking the equipment (tape recorder, camera, etc.) and reviewing previously supplied reference material (interviewee's bio, hotel's press kit, etc.).

3 Start with small talk and simple questions. (Avoid asking

questions that can be answered with a simple *yes* or *no*.)

4 Use body language that says I'm approachable, I'm interested and I'm listening.

5 Don't fear moments of silence. Interviewees may feel the obligation to fill the space; usually the information divulged during this time is valuable to your piece.

6 Obtain the interviewee's business card and ask permission to follow-up by telephone, fax or e-mail with any unanswered questions or to clarify statements.

7 If you must ask a question that may be perceived out of line, save it for the end of the interview. And preface the question with a statement like: 'I don't want this to be interpreted as rude but I think my readers would like to know why ... Could you provide some insight on that?'

8 Be responsible to the interviewee; don't use a statement out of context.

9 Be aware of libel laws and submit your piece accordingly.

10 After publication, send a copy of the piece along with a thank you note to the *expert*.

Inscribe details about the person you're interviewing. Study his demeanour, his style of dress, his surroundings. Does he sit back in his chair and cross his arms as he speaks or lean forward and cup his chin in his hands? Write down anything that will bring the person to life for your readers. (Note that these observations should be made inconspicuously while conducting the interview.)

Text from the article, 'San Diego's Innkeeper: Miss Billy Riley', illustrates the incorporation of these priceless tidbits:

She is especially striking in one of her favorite period dresses, an antique white gown that accents her sparkling blue eyes and silver hair. The white lace parasol in her hand is secured by a tiny pink rosebud, and a double strand of pearls highlights the multi-colored jeweled clasp at her neck.

Continually stopping to chat with guests and to parade her attire, she playfully twirls the parasol. 'Good morning, ladies. Please come and look around. We love to have you here,' she greets newcomers with a welcoming smile.

Be objective but fair

People read travel articles for many reasons. But whether it's for entertainment or for information, it's always for truth. Thus, an additional duty of the travel writer is to be honest, bluntly honest at times, but always fair in your opinions.

This policy of honestly is especially important when free travel is involved. Although we'll discuss press trips and independent itineraries in Chapter 13, let's talk about your creditability when you haven't paid for your travels. Say your hotel stay and air transportation are complimentary – as well as your meals, golf, spa visits, etc. Sounds wonderful, doesn't it? But there is a caveat.

It's your journalistic responsibility to compare your experiences with those of other hotel guests and airline passengers. Was the same courtesy and service universal or was it extended to you as a VIP? How would the average reader be treated? Do all guests receive chocolates at turndown? Is it possible for any restaurant guest to order the specially prepared entree, even though it isn't on the menu? Your job is to explore for answers to questions like these.

Also located in the journalistic responsibility category is the importance of weighing the validity of a single experience. Say you were robbed. Is it a rare episode or a common occurrence? Does the destination have a reputation as a marginally safe area? If so, this information would warrant a 'how to travel safely' sidebar. But if it is an isolated incident, it shouldn't be mentioned.

Is the food in a well-known restaurant typically overrated and overpriced, or was your mediocre meal an anomaly? Find out – it's your job. But it's not your job to attempt to destroy the reputation of an eatery because you had a surly server. Bad service by one employee doesn't necessarily mean the entire staff is terrible. If, however, your second and third visits are met with equal rudeness, you are indebted to your readers to share that while the food may be the best, the waiters may want to read *Miss Manners*.

Beware when your personal trip thermometer registers too hot or too cold. If your travels were absolutely wonderful or positively terrible, step back from the situation. Access the experience objectively, not emotionally; *then* report it.

If, after an unbiased assessment, your travel adventure is still deemed wonderful, ask the staff insightful questions about what could go wrong and how it would be handled. Add this information to your piece.

When the situation is at the opposite end of the good/bad spectrum, determine the cause of an awful encounter. Is it explained by a fluke computer failure or a bout of unseasonably hot or cold weather? Weigh each extreme experience. Your article should reflect ongoing issues and attitudes, not one-time problems.

Address the positives and negatives. I illustrate this advice to my travel writing class by quoting the following letter to the editor. Keep in mind this is not text from a travel article, it's simply an assessment of this traveller's Iranian visit; but it works.

All the scares and fears we anticipated [about Iran] were completely unfounded. We were free to roam the streets at will and enter most religious sites. There are no beggars, and no pesky guides or touts accosted us. The endless bazaars are real, not a string of tourist junk shops. People would light up when we said we were from America. Those who could would approach us to practice their English – the second language in schools. Their very first words were, 'Welcome to our country.'

Iran must be the last bargain on earth. A taxi ride is under a dollar. Dinner for two in a restaurant was [US] $10.

On the negative side: Severe and uncomfortable clothing restrictions are placed on all women, including visitors; the cars and buses are all tired and more than 20 years old; the hotels are clean but the carpets have not been shampooed, the walls not painted and the mattresses and plumbing not replaced since before the revolution. All of this is slowly being rectified, but it will take a long time.

Advice from the master

I notice that you use plain, simple language, short words and brief sentences. This is the way to write English – it is the modern way, and the best way. Stick to it; don't let fluff and flowers and verbosity creep in. When you catch adjectives, kill most of them – then the rest will be valuable. They weaken when they are close together; they give strength when they are wide apart.

Mark Twain, writing to a schoolboy essayist

Dos and don'ts of good writing

Do ...

- Use a noted standard like *Reader's Digest* as a template. (Pattern your work from the best.)
- Write for the reader. (Write as if you're talking to your best friend. Avoid the temptation to impress by using obscure terminology or by talking down to the reader.)
- Slant the piece. (Gear it to your audience – personalize it.)
- Use orthodox punctuation.
- Eliminate the clutter. (Cleaning up a manuscript can be like cleaning a teenager's room.)
- Stop writing when you get to the end.
- Think ahead. (If your country is hosting the Olympics or a nearby city is celebrating its bicentennial in two years, query now.)

Don't ...

- Create a topic too narrow.
- Get wordy.
- Use jargon.
- Force a personal style.
- Explain when you don't have to.
- Pay too much attention to your story – you'll kill it.

Words of writing wisdom

... interview like a pro

Julie Fanselow is a former newspaper reporter and author/co-author of several travel guidebooks. Her titles include *Texas* and *British Columbia* for Lonely Planet, *Traveling the Lewis & Clark Trail* and *Traveling the Oregon Trail* for Falcon Press, as well as *Idaho Off the Beaten Path* for The Globe Pequot Press. In addition, she is a founding member of Guidebookwriters.com, the Internet's top showcase for proven travel-writing talent.

I never end an in-depth interview without asking these two questions:

1 *Is there anything I haven't asked about that you'd like to tell me?*

2 *Of everything you've told me, what's the most important thing you'd like me to report?*

Both these questions are designed to be sure the source fully has his/her say.

As for note-taking, I rely on handwritten notes for most interviews, but I will tape truly in-depth interviews, say, for a personality profile. Don't worry about getting every word down, and abbreviate when you can. Jot a quick star next to the best quotes.

My handwriting is so awful that I'll usually sit down afterward to be sure I can read it (and maybe spell out some words I abbreviated that might be misread later). But when it comes time to write, I don't write my notebook. That is, I keep it closed and write off the top of my head, then return to my notes to fill in facts and exact quotes, etc.

10

writing a book

In this chapter you will learn:
- elements of a book proposal
- how to find the right publisher
- book promotion basics.

She approaches her writing 'sideways, like a horse, starting by writing letters or something and then creeping up on a novel'.

Mary Wesley

After successfully penning articles for publication in newspapers and magazines, the next hurdle of most travel writers is a book. The reasons are varied. The status of becoming an author is certainly appealing. But does the publication of a travel book automatically place the writer on the road to royalty riches? Rarely.

In truth, the book pay scale varies as much as that of the magazine market. And many times the reality is that once expenses for research (including travel costs) are deducted from your profit, it's difficult to yield a significant gain. Yet, the prospect remains enticing and enriching.

Types of travel books

Probably the most visible classification in the travel book category is the guidebook. These are books with names like *Hanging Out in Europe* and *Culture Shock! Malaysia*. Guidebooks are objectively written manuals covering the details of a destination's well-known highlights, little known sites, hotels, restaurants, transportation, etc.

Other types of travel books include general travel information (*I'll Never Get Lost Again: The Complete Guide to Improving Your Sense of Direction*), niche travel (*Kids' New York*), how-to travel books (*10 Minute Guide to Travel Planning on the Net*), special interest (*The Independent Walker's Guide to Italy*) and coffee table books (*The Great Cities/Dublin*).

The travel book list is incomplete without the inclusion of the travel essay. This type of writing tells the story of actual people in actual places. Frances Mayes penned a travel book when she wrote *Under the Tuscan Sun*, as did Peter Mayle in his recount of the restoration of a 200-year-old farm house in *A Year in Provence*. One of the profession's most celebrated travel essayists, of course, is Mark Twain – author of *Following the Equator*, *Life on the Mississippi* and *The Innocents Abroad* (covering a 1867 trip to Europe and the Holy Land).

Slant for the sale

Is there a market for it? Will it sell? In short, does your book have commercial value? These are the questions you must answer in your initial contact with a book editor. The best way to entice this decision maker is to hook him with a summary phrase or title about a topic slanted for maximum appeal.

My research for this chapter included a bookstore visit where I collected titles like *The Cheapskate's Guide to Las Vegas* and *What the Airlines Never Tell You* – titles that define the book's audience (budget and air travellers in these respective publications). It is important to define an audience as clearly as these two examples do because publishers want to know who the potential buyers are and where to reach them.

Brainstorm the marketing options. Is there potential for the book to be used at learning institutions (*Teach Yourself Travel Writing*), for travel agency or tour operator giveaways (*The Real Guide to Portugal*), as bridal gifts (*Hawaii's Favourite Honeymoon Spots*)? Can it be sold at specialty stores like wine emporiums (*Napa Valley's Oldest Wineries*) or for holidays such as Valentine's Day (*The World's Top Ten Cities for Kissing*)? Your initiative in identifying these potential markets will identify you as a serious author and will exponentially increase your chances of being published.

Study the competition

Before you commit extensive time in the development of the book proposal or the project itself, study your competition. This assignment can be accomplished in several ways. It's as simple as a visit to the library or bookstore to see who is publishing the kind of book you envisage writing.

The purpose of your visit is to answer questions like these. How many books are there on your subject? When were they published (recently or several years ago)? How would your book differ from these? What would your book include that these books do not? Now it's time to take notes. Write down the trim size (the physical dimensions) of each book, number of pages and description of the cover.

Note that larger bookstores may be more valuable because they will have many of the most recent releases; several of a library's books on the subject may be checked out. Don't neglect the library, however, because a good librarian will be able to suggest reference resources that list most books in print. While this option won't allow you to see physical copies of competitive books, you will have their titles.

Prospect for publishers

Search out likely publishers for your book. Seek those that produce books in your genre. Remember the investigative techniques from Chapter 06 – matching periodicals with magazine articles? Follow these procedures. They vary somewhat, but the basics are the same. Once again, your goal is similar – to produce a query (and/or proposal) that targets the most appropriate publisher.

Contact these publishing houses and request their most recent catalogue or go to booksellers' conferences and collect them. A publication's catalogue lists all the books the publisher sells. (This information may also be provided on individual Web sites.) Study individual catalogues to determine if your book would meet a publisher's needs. After perusing the catalogue and Web site (if available), you may find it simply would not be a good match.

But you will uncover several good matches and once you do, it's time to turn to sources that index publishers. This list is a familiar one. It includes *Writer's Market, International Writers' & Artists' Yearbook* (UK version of *Writer's Market*), *Literary Market Place, International Literary Market Place* and *Writer's Guide to Book Editors, Publishers and Literary Agents*.

The next steps are reminiscent of those discussed in the Chapter 06 topic, 'Study marketing manuals'. Each book publisher listing will have information like:

1 address
2 telephone, fax, and e-mail information
3 name of submissions/acquistions editor
4 types of books they publish
5 compensation details
6 policy on unagented and multiple submissions
7 tips on query and proposal submissions
8 response time

The following is a partial listing found in *Writer's Market* for Pelican Publishing Company: non-fiction – travel (regional and international); publishes 70 titles/year; receives 5000 submissions/ year; 15% of books from first time authors; 90% from unagented writers; pays royalty on actual receipts; no multiple queries or submissions; reviews artwork/photos as part of ms package.

Review these book publisher listings, just as you did for the magazine market, and note the relevant information in each one you deem a *possibility*; then evaluate your slate of choices. Remember to choose wisely – your selection may become a long-term partner.

Suggestions for having a 'happy marriage'

Eva Shaw, author of *Writing the Nonfiction Book* (Rodgers & Nelsen Publishing Co.), likens the union between a writer and his agent and/or publisher to a marriage. Here are some of her suggestions for achieving a *happy* one:

Keep your promises. *And remind those involved if their promises are not met.*

Meet all your deadlines.

Produce the book that you've proposed.

Be willing to compromise. *You'll have to give 150% (just like in a marriage) and be willing to overlook the problems that arise, because they will.*

Work like your book is going to be a bestseller. *Expect your publisher and agent to do so too.*

Be available. *Return phone calls and e-mail.*

Follow up on suggestions. *Make the changes that need to be done.*

Don't be a pest. *No matter how anxious you are, calling agents and publishers more than necessary will not endear you to them.*

What about the query?

Once again I answer the *query versus no query* question by looking at my watch. In the same way that I regard it a time consideration to send a query before submitting a magazine article, I suggest that you query a publisher prior to mailing a book proposal. When you consider the time it takes to complete a proposal or write a book, query letters become an even greater time management tool. Remember to keep detailed records of whom and where you send your queries, along with their responses.

Book proposal

When your query elicits a positive response from a book editor, it's time to write the proposal. Because nearly all non-fiction books are contracted by publishers on the strength of the proposal itself – not the completed book – this written presentation is crucial. Note that you shouldn't even think of approaching an agent until you have written a proposal.

The assemblage of a book proposal, which includes at least one sample chapter, is without doubt a time-consuming endeavour. But it is time well spent because a well-conceived, fully developed book proposal becomes a blueprint to follow when it's time to write the book.

A non-fiction book proposal should contain the following elements.

Cover letter

Use the best opener or hook you can write.

This letter should concisely list the pertinent main points and the most compelling highlights of your book.

Notify the editor if you are sending multiple queries, which is acceptable as long as you state so in your letter. (The exception to the multiple query rule is if the publication specifies otherwise.)

Include the completion date. Be specific and don't make promises you will be unable to meet.

Title page

Include the working title, your name, address and phone number.

Proposal table of contents

List every component included in the *proposal* (not the proposed book).

Complete this table of contents *after* the proposal has been written.

Book overview

- *Concept*: Address the book's overall theme and highlight its strongest features.
- *Marketing information*: Include facts about how and to whom your book can be successfully marketed. This information is now expected to accompany every book proposal. (Note that the inclusion of additional data like potential audience demographics will increase your chances of acceptance.)
- *Competition*: Write a one- to two-sentence synopsis of each book against which yours would compete; address how yours is different and better.
- *Physical characteristics*: Cover the basics: number of pages, the inclusion of pictures or illustrations (remember colour increases print costs), book size (standard size is 9″ × 6″; deviations can decrease the interest by bookstores), the incorporation of Web site addresses, references, glossaries, appendices, etc.

Author information

Acquaint the editor with your writing background. Include an author's bio.

Convince the editor of your qualifications to write about the subject.

Chapter outline

Treat this as a detailed table of contents.

This element consists of a traditional outline, or more often, a short paragraph describing each chapter.

Representative sample chapter(s)

Send at least one perfected sample chapter (more if they request). This work must be your very best.

Attachments

Include clips of magazine articles; preferably about the topic. (Never send originals.)

Send an SAE.

Note that if your proposal is rejected by several publishers – and they all say the same thing – you may want to revise it accordingly before submitting elsewhere.

Agent?

An agent is your personal representative with the publisher. The reason writers work with agents is simple: they want to spend time writing, not shopping their book or negotiating a contract (many times a better contract). Thus, agented writers consider the fee – usually 10 to 15% of the money their book generates – money well spent.

Getting an agent, however, is much like finding your first job. It's the old *how do you get a job (an agent) with no experience (a book)* versus *how do you get experience (a book) with no job (an agent)* dilemma.

How do you find an agent? The best place to start is with colleagues, writing instructors, local authors and members of writers' groups. Ask them the following questions. Do you have or know of a good agent? What do you or don't you like about your agent? What is your agent's fee? (Are there charges for telephone calls or other incidentals?)

Once again, sources can be *Literary Market Place, International Literary Market Place, Writer's Market, International Writers' & Artists' Yearbook* and *Writer's Guide to Book Editors, Publishers and Literary Agents* – references that list literary agencies. (You may also refer to the following table of helpful Web sites in this search.) And never neglect the reference-checking procedure when you come to the final stages of the selection process. (Check just as you would a prospective employee's references.)

Be aware that some literary agents, as well as publishing houses, charge a fee to review a writer's work. Sometimes this is a charge for a legitimate service; other times it is not. Before you invest in a reader's fee, it is wise to check the credentials of the agency or publishing house. A more frugal approach, however, might be to take a writing class at a local university or join a writer's critique group.

Web sites helpful to the book author

Directory of Literary Agents
An on-line directory of literary agents who do not charge reading fees.
www.writers.net/agents.php

Publishers' Catalogues Home Page
Lists catalogues of publishers everywhere.
www.lights.com/publisher/

Sensible Solutions
Offers advice on marketing your work, looking for a publisher and self-publishing.
www.happilypublished.com

Writer's Federation of Nova Scotia
Advice on writing a non-fiction book proposal.
www.chebucto.ns.ca/Culture/WFNS/booknfic.html

In today's world of publishing, the large number of submissions versus a book editor's time has resulted in many publishing houses accepting only agented material. Hence, the logical assumption is that agents are indispensable. But as with most suppositions, this one is not always true.

Contemplate the following informal research that I conducted by evaluating a randomly selected page of *Writer's Market*. Four publishers were listed on the page. The results: publisher 1 accepts 95% from unagented writers, publisher 2 accepts 100% from unagented writers, publisher 3 accepts 100% from unagented writers and publisher 4 accepts 90% from unagented writers. Consider this information, check your own reference sources – then evaluate your personal needs to make the determination whether or not an agent is right for you.

Money *matters*

The words *advance* and *royalty* will become familiar ones once you've entered the book publishing world. Advance is the amount a publisher pays a writer before a book is published; it is deducted from the royalties earned from sales of the finished book. Royalty is a percentage of the amount received from retail sales of a book; it is paid to the author by the publisher.

No standard can be applied to the amount of an advance you can expect to receive. Many times you may be offered a very modest sum, even no advance. But don't despair because the smaller the advance, the sooner it will be paid out of your royalties and the sooner those royalty cheques will arrive in the mail.

Indemnity clause

An indemnity clause assures a guarantee from you that the work is yours; that the work is original. The inclusion of this provision in your contract is standard – you'll find it in all book contracts.

Should you fail to abide by the indemnity clause by declining to obtain permission to use a photo or a portion of another writer's work, for example, you will be responsible for the payment of legal fees and any expenses incurred by the publisher because of this mistake. Thus, the importance of abiding by the indemnity clause translates into both your money and reputation.

Contract negotiation

While a first-time book author may wield little leverage on the negotiation scene, there are certain elements to address before signing the dotted line. It never hurts to ask for: a larger advance, larger percentage in royalties, negotiation of subsidiary rights (movie rights and electronic book rights, for instance), a greater number of free copies, provision to buy copies at a steep discount to sell at lectures, conferences, etc., a deadline extension (if you think you'll need it) and financial assistance in the marketing effort.

The final but most important portion of negotiation advice is to have an attorney well versed in publishing law review the contract before you sign it. His fee is worth the investment, not to mention your peace of mind.

Dealing with deadlines

Deadlines? Once again, you don't miss them; this is why it's important to set a realistic one. Remember you've signed a contract. Not making your deadline may invalidate your contract *and* you will be expected to return the advance.

If missing a deadline is unavoidable, the only way to handle the situation is to be honest with your editor and to divulge this truth as far in advance of the expected delivery date as possible.

Manuscript preparation

In spite of the mammoth technological advances we have experienced over the last few years, most publishing houses still expect the same manuscript format they have received for decades. Standard tips include:

- Check and double-check your manuscript for typographical and grammatical errors.
- Double-space your manuscript. Use easy-to-read (no script) 12-point font.
- Don't bind your manuscript. Use a folding clip.
- Use 20-pound (minimum) white bond paper.
- Do indent paragraphs.
- Do not justify the right margin.
- Leave about 1-inch on all margins (top, bottom, left and right).
- *Always* keep a copy for your records.

Note that many publishers will have their own formatting requirements, for example no indented paragraphs, no use of tabs, one space (not two) between sentences. Follow whatever specific instructions your publisher requests.

Self-publishing

Self-publishing is just what it sounds like. You do everything yourself: clerical duties, editing tasks, printing chores, promotional work. In this arrangement, you keep all the income derived from the book, but you also pay for its entire cost – from its production to its promotion.

While self-publishing was once considered a sub-standard means of getting a book in the marketplace, many happily choose this path. A number of lecturers, business professionals and specialists on the speaking engagement circuit find self-publishing a lucrative way to sell books to a ready-made audience.

It's time to promote

Gone are the days when your publisher will set up a promotional tour, book your arrangements and whisk you around the world to help sell your tome. This VIP treatment is reserved for the few once-in-a-lifetime writers at the top. Thus, much of the promotion is up to you. Here are some suggestions:

• Contact reviewers/media. Call the publishing house and speak to the individual responsible for publicity. Ask about publicity plans. Have book reviewers been contacted? If so, follow up with a phone call. If not, which is likely the case, send a brief note along with a copy of the book (hopefully the publisher will provide these copies) to a selection of reviewers.

What about appropriate television and radio programmes? If your publisher hasn't made the initiative, send a press kit, a letter telling why your appearance on their programme will benefit their audience and an SAE along with your phone number and e-mail address to appropriate media outlets.

Your press kit should include:

1 a professional black and white photograph of yourself
2 a personal bio
3 a press release on the book
4 clips of publicity
5 a book facts sheet
6 your book or a colour copy of the book's cover (in absence of the book).

• Publicize yourself. Ask your publisher to send you pre-printed flyers advertising the book (including purchase details). An alternative is to request a four-colour glossy of the book cover from the publisher. Use this glossy as artwork and design your own promotional handout. These promotional pieces can range from one-page handouts to postcards and bookmarks.

• Network. Create an extensive list with names of business associates, friends, family, neighbours and members of writing organizations. Forward this list to your publicity contact, with the request to send promotional fliers. If this inquiry isn't possible, complete the task yourself. Then send ten extra handouts to each person on your list and ask if they will distribute them to their local libraries and bookstores.

- Arrange book signings. Contact bookstores and request book signings. (Many of your local vendors will welcome the opportunity to show off a hometown author.) And don't forget to place one of your bookmarks inside each book you sell at the signing – to spread the word even further.

- Contact catalogues. Peruse and use the potential of the catalogue market. Catalogue sales have mushroomed over the past several years. If you come across a directory that would be a good fit for your book, call the catalogue's sales department. Ask for the name of the appropriate contact person; then write an enticing sales letter and send a book.

Words of writing wisdom

... it's in the detail

Elizabeth Hansen's travel writing career began in 1978 with sales of articles to *San Diego Magazine* (in her home town) and the *Los Angeles Times*. She continues to write for periodicals, but has also authored numerous guidebooks – mostly in the Frommer series – becoming a New Zealand/Australia specialist.

I think one reason I've been successful is that I was a traveller long before I was a travel writer, so I know what readers need. With guidebooks, long descriptions of the scenery are pretty much a waste of space. The readers will see the sunset, skyline, etc. when they get there. What they need from a travel guide is honest, down-to-earth advice so they can plan their itineraries, calculate their travel budgets and possibly make advance reservations.

I tend to be very detail oriented, so this type of writing is a natural for me. For every book project, I develop forms to be completed on site. For instance, when I wrote Bed & Breakfast New Zealand *I had a three-page questionnaire that I completed at each B&B I visited. That way I was sure I had all the information I needed and could weave these facts into my description of each place as I wrote the book.*

For the Frommer guides, in addition to the forms for places to stay, places to eat, sightseeing attractions and so forth, I also created a checklist for each locale. This helped me make sure I had all the information I needed on a particular city or town before I moved on.

I love writing about New Zealand and Australia, but one drawback is that if you forget to check something out when you're there, it's a long way to go back.

Words of writing wisdom

... a guide to guidebooks

Katharine Dyson is author of two books, *The 100 Best Romantic Resorts of the World* and *The Finger Lakes Book: A Complete Guide*. She also served as the consultant for A&E television programme's, 'Top 10 Romantic Destinations'.

My guidebook writing was launched when Kay Showker, author of 100 Best Caribbean Resorts, *told me her publisher, Globe Pequot Press, was looking for an author to write a new book. I followed up on the lead and got the job to write* 100 Best Romantic Resorts of the World, *now in its 3rd edition.*

My most recent book, The Finger Lakes Book: A Complete Guide, *came to me another way. After receiving a guidebook in the mail to review for my travel column and impressed by the quality of the writing and format, I contacted Berkshire House, the publisher, and asked if they would be interested in a guidebook to the Finger Lakes for their Great Destination series.*

Since I had grown up in the region, the subject was close to my heart. After several months of checking the viability of such a book, and discovering that there was no reference of that kind in the marketplace, they agreed to do it.

One thing I've learned, if you kept track of the hours required for thoroughly researching and writing a guidebook and then figured out what you're getting per hour, you would probably commit suicide. If you're in it for the money, don't do it. If you want to gain credibility as a serious, published travel writer and feel you will gain a great deal of satisfaction in having a book you've written in the marketplace, then go for it.

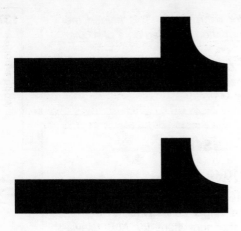

avoid the pitfalls

Whether you're writing travel articles or travel books, it's a tough gig. You spend a lot of time away from home. You usually work under the significant pressure of deadlines for an insignificant amount of money. And you're competing against some of the best.

But don't misinterpret the purpose of this chapter. Make no mistake: it is not meant to discourage, but rather to encourage. So pay heed to the following advice. Its intention is to propel you over the pitfalls.

Marinate, percolate, whatever

The absolute first thing to do when you launch a writing project is to resist the impulse to start writing. You need to relax, to settle down and above all you need to think. Don't worry about wasting time; it's never a waste of time to get your thoughts in order.

Herbert E. Meyer and Jill M. Meyer

Assemble your senses. Take the time to meditate and contemplate, appraise and access, remember and reminisce. Whether you call it marinating or percolating, its purpose is to ready the writer to *write*.

Every writer has his own routine for this stage of the writing process. I liken it to letting a fine bottle of wine sit and age, rather than opening it prematurely. It's simply a necessary step in the process to perfection.

This is the time to review your photography. Listen to tapes of native music. Surround yourself with souvenirs bought as mementos, even the tacky ones. Look at your notes again – fill in the blanks. Examine the collected press kits and brochures; peruse them carefully, highlight them. Pull out the encyclopedia and see what it says about the locale or subject. Indulge in a novel set in the destination.

Feed this cornucopia of information into your subconscious. Set the material aside for a day or two; then put up your antennae. It's important to be ready to intercept the dominant theme or sentiment that repeatedly comes to mind, because this info usually points you in the direction your story or book should go.

In writing you have to be married to your unconscious. You choose a time and say, 'I'll meet you there tomorrow', and your unconscious prepares something for you.

Norman Mailer

A word of caution is to *resist* the urge to short circuit this process. If you're under a looming deadline, you may consider this time spent a frivolous folly. I assure you, it isn't. Don't follow the path behind the frantic, panicked travel writer who cheats himself and ultimately his readers of a thoughtful, multi-dimensional piece of work.

Percolate but don't procrastinate

Doing everyday things like dusting the house, baking bread and going to the movies – while contemplating ideas – is not all bad. I call this percolation. But beware of the distinct difference between percolation and procrastination.

An unfortunate learned behaviour from our school days is to procrastinate – put off starting a major project until the combination of fear and the clock produces enough adrenaline to begin. Some writers flourish from this approach and from the panic created by questioning whether or not a deadline can be met. The downside, however, is that while this course can be stimulating, it can also be incapacitating.

Get in the creative flow

Described as a runner's high, this happening occurs when a writer begins to write *effortlessly*. I liken this enviable experience to strenuously pumping a bicycle uphill in order to coast down it.

Getting in this creative flow has been described in a number of ways:

An altered condition when you look at your writing and say, 'Wow, I wrote that!'
A trance-like state where time is meaningless – you forget to eat; you don't need to sleep.
A writing frenzy where creativity is flowing too fast to edit yourself.

How do you get in the creative flow? Advice varies. One writer will say, 'Don't try to force yourself into it; ease into it.' Another will advise setting a goal – whether it's a rough outline, a title, a lead, a first paragraph. All agree that the writing tool (i.e. computer, typewriter or pencil and paper) must match the writer. However, the most valuable advice is simply to put the pen to the paper; or as Nike ads urge, *Just Do It.*

Get black on white.

Guy de Maupassant

One component most writers agree upon is the importance of establishing a work day ritual. My ritual is to start my day around 5.30 am by exercising. (Endorphins get the creative juices flowing.) After breakfast I begin to assemble my particular needs: glass of water, fine-point red pen (for editing), radio set on favourite station, a lit aromatic candle.

But once I'm sitting in front of my computer screen, I experience a Pavlovian reaction – it's time to write. I'm not saying I always want to work or that I'm even ready to do so; but I know that's why I'm at my desk. There's no right or wrong routine. It doesn't even matter what routine you have, as long as it's a routine.

Whether it's a commitment to write 1500 or 2000 words each day or to work for a set number of hours, it's important to incorporate structure into a potentially unstructured job.

How do the masters do it? *Memoirs of a Geisha* author, Arthur Golden, works toward a daily goal: to write 2000 words (takes approximately six hours). Olivia Goldsmith, author of *First Wives' Club*, writes four hours every day (from 8 am to 12 noon), eats lunch, then spends about an hour editing the previous day's work. Julia Cameron, who penned and teaches creative methods found in *The Artist's Way*, urges the daily commitment to *morning pages* – defined as three pages of longhand writing (strictly stream of consciousness).

Work like a writer

Set your own realistic daily, monthly or annual goals. Define productivity in your terms – by a pre-determined schedule that corresponds to your personal work style, experience and available time. By definition of the name *freelance*, you're a writer who may accept or decline assignments. So why not aim for the pace that suits you, you may wonder. Would goals then be necessary?

I believe goals are always necessary. They help both mentally and tangibly. When I embarked on this book, my longest writing project to date (50,000 words), I calculated the number of words I would need to produce each day in order to be finished by deadline.

Keep in mind that it was necessary to squeeze my book writing days between my committed travel days and the completion of other projects so it was a tremendous challenge. But after several weeks of working on the book exclusively, I easily upped my daily production.

When my horse is running good, I don't stop to give him sugar.

William Faulkner

As part of the bargain I made with myself, once I completed my daily quota, I could leave the computer and go to the beach, to a friend's house, to a comfortable chair with a good novel or wherever – and to go with a clear conscience. For me this approach has always been the secret to reaching my goals and meeting the needs of editors and publishers.

To outline or not to outline?

Think of a person talking who interrupts to address another subject, then returns to the original topic, drifts to an unrelated aside, introduces an additional theme and wanders from that one as well. Confusing, isn't it?

How can you avoid a similarly confusing scenario on paper? When a piece doesn't play out in words as you mentally envisioned, it's usually because you didn't take sufficient time to organize. Whether organization means brainstorming, clustering (bubbling), outlining or blocking an article – or a combination of any of these methods – matters not. What matters is to select an organizational process compatible with your learning style; one that gets your thoughts in order.

Recognized as one of the best tools for generating ideas, brainstorming results in unscripted, multi-dimensional thinking. It's nothing more than giving your mind the licence to play with and embellish an idea.

Effective brainstorming includes certain elements:

1 There is no right or wrong thinking process – *everything* is a potential idea.

2 Hand write ideas (a list generated on a computer uses a different, less spontaneous mental process).

3 Write as fast as you can (speed is the catalyst for creativity).

On the other end of the spectrum is the outline. Outlines aren't as challenging as many believe them to be if they are approached as a non-judgmental tool. An outline serves the same purpose as a mission statement – it helps you focus on exactly what your article or book is about and assists in arranging your ideas in a logical pattern.

One of the values of outlining a large writing project is found in the sub-sections. (These sub-topics become a travel writer's checklist; they ensure you haven't forgotten or duplicated a subject.) As a rule, the more complicated and lengthy the project – like a book – the more critical an outline becomes.

Clustering or bubbling, as it's sometimes called, is a non-intimidating outline alternative. This method is less structured; it resembles a child's elementary drawing and the entire process takes about ten minutes.

Very simply it consists of the article's topic (two to three words) printed and circled in the centre of a large piece of paper. Ten to 12 surrounding circles (connected by lines to the centre cluster) represent sub-topics.

The concept is to write ideas in each of these circles quickly, generating possibility after possibility. To continue the process a step further and develop one of these sub-topics, place its name in the centre of another piece of paper, circle it and repeat the cluster exercise.

Writer's block

There's absolutely no way to prevent an attack of 'writer's fatigue.' It's like the flu; when it hits, it hits ... your concentration begins to flag, you lose your mental focus and for a moment can't remember what point you were trying to make ... Accept the attack for what it is, and take a break ... put your writing project out of mind – read a spy novel, paint the garage, ride your bike, listen to music, go to a movie. Just remember that taking a break to clear the cobwebs out of your brain and to recharge your batteries is part and parcel of the writing process.

Herbert E. Meyer and Jill M. Meyer

There are as many theories on writer's block as there are writers who have experienced it. But whether this writing malady is the result of fear of failure, overwork, lack of stimulation or a number of other reasons, it's important to forestall the paralysis it inflicts.

It's probably best to approach writer's block through preventive measures. A few ways to avert this dilemma are:

1 Start your day by turning on your computer.
2 Find your peak time and use it well; set writing hours (no phone calls, no dentist appointments, no library visits).
3 Give yourself *easy* deadlines.

Following the practice of Ernest Hemingway has always helped me. The prolific author found it easier to start writing if on the preceding day he stopped in the middle of a sentence. His theory was that instead of agonizing over what should come next, he would just complete the unfinished sentence and continue writing.

But after writer's block has struck, journalists prescribe an assortment of treatments. One extreme resolution is to remain seated at the computer, staring at it for hours if necessary, even if the end result is the composition of only a few words. Kinder remedies follow for the hopelessly blocked.

Working through writer's block

- Re-read or rewrite a portion of what you've written.
- Make a list of things to do in order to finish the piece.
- Research a bit more. You may not have enough information to cover the subject properly. (But don't use this second research process endlessly to postpone facing the manuscript.)
- Eliminate both physical and mental clutter. Teachers of young children will say a disorganized study environment is not conducive to organized thoughts. And mental clutter is equally destructive. (Author Julia Cameron says to write what's bothering you on paper and set it aside.)
- Review your notes, your research, your written work. Digest it; set it aside (let your own personal computer called *your mind* fine tune your project).
- Take a break and get away from it (take a walk, work in the garden, play a set of tennis). Read a motivational book. (One of my favourites is Natalie Goldberg's *Writing Down the Bones.*)

Think small

The first item on a beginner's agenda is get published – *anywhere, for any price, on any subject*; there's no substitute for publication. How do you think small?

Until you have a clip or two in your portfolio, submit where it's safe. Forget the top-name consumer magazines for now; and put off writing the book for a while. Don't think in terms of money (larger payments will come later). Avoid publications that expect a highly polished query letter. Instead, send completed articles to smaller magazines that read unsolicited manuscripts – publications where your chances for a sale are good.

The reasoning behind this exception to the *query rule* follows. The beginner's writing world is different from the world of the established writer. More than likely, the novice is not yet in the category of writers who regularly sell an idea or get a manuscript read on the strength of a compelling query. Of course, the beginner significantly multiplies his chances by first studying the market and reading past copies of the magazines he is targeting.

Write about what you know

Because beginners usually write part time and don't have the time to research a subject in depth, the best starting point is to write about something you know, something you do frequently, something around the corner.

As a Southern California resident I am surrounded by potential travel stories – Tijuana (Mexico), beaches, mountains, Hollywood, Palm Springs desert area, Disneyland and more. These places are my haunts. I visit them frequently.

And coupled with these distinctive locales come their corresponding activities: dining, sunbathing, sailing, snowmobiling, sightseeing, jeeping. This is a good start for the beginner. It was for me and remains so. To this day, much of what I write pertains to things *I know* – shopping, travelling with children, golf.

Specializing makes sense

'We are most interested in writers with a special expertise to bring to the travel experience, i.e. architecture, theater, snowboarding, etc.', says one publication in its tips found in *Writer's Market*.

This one-sentence statement echoes the priority most periodicals attach to specialization. Why is a premium placed on writing about what you love? Editors have found that the best writing is the result of an author's personal passion. (See Words of writing wisdom at the end of this chapter.)

Answer the following questions and you're on the way to uncovering *your* potential specialties. What do you like? How do you travel? Why do you travel? What is it you look for in a trip? Do you just want to relax and get away from it all or do you want to immerse yourself in a foreign culture and destination? Do you want to see every museum, or do you want to eat your way around the country?

You may consider specializing in a geographical area. I've worked with writers who have become experts in the Caribbean, Mexico and the Pacific Rim. But not all travel writing is about destinations. Many writers have a particular area of expertise. For years I have written about the meetings industry. It's a big business and it's conducted around the world.

Other areas of specialization might be: business travel, honeymoon travel, soft adventure travel or family travel. As my children grew up, my story angles changed. Concentrating on family-oriented pieces, my articles ranged from cruising with young children to successful travel with a teen – based on a Hawaiian trip with my 16-year-old daughter, Erin.

Maybe you're a photographer and can write for photo magazines or you can compose a weekly newspaper column for the camera buff. Say you're a world-class downhill skier; concentrate on the sport and winter ski resorts. A former cruise line employee will have specialized knowledge of this industry and can write an insider's book or consumer column for seafaring travellers.

Don't reject rejects

All beginning freelancers should expect rejection slips. My advice to you is: expect them, but don't accept them. Here's how to turn this perceived negative into a positive. When a returned manuscript is accompanied by words of encouragement, consider it a favourable reject; then follow up on it.

One fruitful writer shared this statistic: over 95% of everything he's sold in his career has been rejected at least twice before a sale. Remember this statistic – resubmit and resubmit often. Editors will tell you what kind of manuscripts they seek. Here's what one editor penned on my 'Climbing Diamond Head' manuscript:

> *The subject caught our attention. After going over the story several times and with the input of the news editor – with whom I select our lead (cover page) articles – we've decided to pass on this one. In short, this is why: the focus of the piece – the hike and its rewards – is rather lost under rather flowery and distracting observations.*

I followed the advice he generously shared and subsequently sold the piece. The lesson is clear. Writers, especially newcomers, should consider a rejection with a favourable comment as a *near sale*. Then he should rework and resubmit it, not set it aside – before tackling a new project.

Follow the editor's direction, whatever it may be. Slice the prose, as I did in the Diamond Head piece, if so advised. If an editor rejects your manuscript because it's longer than the publication's standard stories, cut it and resubmit it. When the editor says he has an abundance of back inventory (accompanied with a 'try us again in a few months' notation), mark it on your calendar. Should an editor reject your idea due to competing projects, this means your basic idea is on target but your timing is off. Resubmit it to other publications.

Follow through, follow up and keep following

Say you've mailed your letter-perfect manuscript, accompanied by clips and a cover letter, to a publication. According to the writer's guidelines, you can expect a response in two months. But it's been 12 weeks and you have received no word.

What is your next step? You have two options:

1 Send a manuscript status letter (accompanied by an SASE (SAE)).
2 Telephone.

Neither approach is right or wrong but each should be accompanied by common sense. (See the following sample letter.)

Sample manuscript status letter

Dear Ms. Ford:

This letter serves as an inquiry regarding the status of my 1500-word article entitled *'Title'*, which was sent to you for consideration <u>(date).</u> It has been several months since the submission and as I have not yet received a response from you, I would appreciate you taking a minute to complete the following checklist.

Your assistance in this matter will help in my tracking process and enable me to send the piece to other outlets should it not be appropriate for your editorial needs.

__ Your story will be published <u>(date).</u>

__ Your story remains under consideration.

__ Your story is on file for possible future use.

__ We do not read unsolicited mss.

__ We have no record of your submission. Please resubmit.

__ Other. _____

Thank you for your response.

Sincerely,

Cynthia Dial

Should you decide to telephone, incorporate these tips: keep it brief; be prepared with manuscript details (title, date sent, name of editor sent to, subjects covered); don't argue with a *no* verdict and if (but *only if*) the editor seems receptive, ask how you can tailor the piece to his exact needs.

In the same way that you follow up with favourable rejects, follow up your successes. Once you've been published by a editor or book publisher, contact him again. Query with new ideas. He's recognized your work as saleable; he likes your writing style. Operate by the time-worn saying: 'Strike while the iron is hot.'

Remember the law of averages. One writer may query a new idea every time he submits a completed manuscript. Another may consider Monday *query day* and pen a new letter of inquiry at the beginning of each week.

Following is advice that writer Ray Bradbury (author of *Fahrenheit 451* and *Zen in the Art of Writing*) gave attendees at a writer's conference: 'The key is to write a lot. Write 52 articles a year. I dare you to write 52 bad ones.'

The deal about deadlines

If there's no deadline, I create a self-imposed one. I may promise a piece to an editor by a certain date to establish a commitment on my part, and I keep that promise because I don't like breaking my word. In this business it's unprofessional at best and at worst – it's deadly.

'If you don't make your deadlines, you won't get off square one in your writing career,' says freelancer Katharine Dyson:

> First you have to establish your priorities. I have a very simple way of doing this. I write each article I am assigned into a calendar on the day it's due and circle it in red. As I complete each piece, I cross it out. I like doing this. It gives me a sense I'm keeping on top of things.
>
> I also write down the specific days I plan to devote to a particular project. This helps keep me focused. I break down large projects like guidebooks into parts or chapters and give myself deadlines to complete each component. Working backwards from the due date, I allocate enough days to complete the assignment.

Networking and self-promotion

Don't neglect the importance of face-to-face encounters. Make the time to attend press gatherings so you can personally meet newspaper and magazine decision makers. An editor/writer relationship is only enhanced when each can put a name to a face. The same is true in the world of book publishing. Attend writers' conferences; introduce yourself to publishers and agents alike.

You'll meet and work with other writers, travel editors, public relations representatives, hotel publicists, airline executives and tourist board delegates, among others, in both your travels and in the course of your research. Who you know is as important in travel writing as it is in other professions, so collect business cards and cultivate these professional relationships.

Join professional organizations. Whether a group is geared to the writer or the travel professional, membership in these associations gives legitimacy and creditability to the travel journalist, especially the beginner. Invitations from public relations firms and national tourist organizations may be extended as the result of membership in some of these organizations. Of course, free or financially assisted trips are only extended to writers with assignments or those with a substantial history of published work.

One of my standard New Year's resolutions is to contact editors on my *publication wish list* for the purpose of introducing myself, my work and my desire to write for them. Thus, at the beginning of each year I send letters of introduction and a selection of pertinent samples of my work to a number of editors. Some editors never respond. Others have – with an assignment.

Some writers like myself (www.travelwritingbycynthiadial) use the Internet to promote themselves and their work. They have a home page, detailing their background and experience and perhaps showcase a sample of their work. Their Web site is included on their letterhead and CV, and reference to the Web site is sometimes used in lieu of providing a bio.

Ways to avoid the pitfalls

A baker's dozen

1 Always maintain professionalism (whether on the phone or on the road).
2 Work toward and achieve goals.
3 Aim high.
4 Deliver and display a positive attitude.
5 Offer a firm handshake; make eye contact; smile.
6 Be dependable. (Meet deadlines, keep your word, fulfil promises – whether to sources, editors, colleagues.)
7 Be trustworthy. (Remain true to your readers; be fair to your destination or subject.)
8 Ascribe to the law of averages. Query, query, query.
9 Stay in good mental and physical health.
10 Don't think of yourself as an island – network.
11 Follow up and follow through with contacts.
12 Continue to learn. (Take classes, read books, become a master of your profession.)
13 Never get discouraged.

Words of writing wisdom

... write about what you love

Roger Cox began his career as a freelance travel writer in 1979 after several years of freelance editorial work for the Fodor and Frommer series of travel guidebooks. He went on to write two books of his own, *The World's Best Tennis Vacations* and *The Best Places to Stay in the Rockies*. He has also written hundreds of articles for *Tennis* magazine, the *Robb Report*, *New Choices*, *Arthur Frommer's Budget Travel*, *Diversion* and *USTA Magazine*, among others. Along the way he launched his own Web site, Tennis Resorts Online (www.tennisresortsonline.com), to help tennis-playing vacationers find the best resort or camp for their needs.

Among the first pieces of advice I received was to write about subjects I cared passionately about. For me, one of those was – and remains – tennis, and so early in my career I approached Tennis *magazine with several ideas for travel stories. In order to know what to pitch, I had gone back over the previous two years of issues, first to find out what sorts of travel stories they used, and second to ensure that I did not suggest something they'd already written about. To my delight, they agreed to a feature on tennis in Hawaii, giving me a deadline of six months later and apologizing for only being able to pay me US $300 (this was 1981).*

Two weeks later, however, I got a call from the managing editor asking whether I was available to go on assignment to Mexico (the writer who was scheduled to go had backed out). Then once I completed that assignment, they sent me to Florida. By the time I finally wrote the Hawaii story, they had asked me to become a contributing editor and had bumped feature fees up to US $750.

Meanwhile, I was vigorously pitching other magazines not only about tennis but also skiing (I grew up in Colorado), canoeing, biking, snorkelling, scuba diving, white water rafting and a host of other outdoor activities. I pursued these partly because I myself liked active vacations, and partly because they seemed to be easy stories to market. Often those stories provided an introduction to an editor and once that relationship was established it became much easier to secure other, more general travel assignments, and ultimately took me to such exotic destinations as Nepal, the Ivory Coast, Bangkok and Bali.

But I continued to look for ways to solidify my relationship with Tennis *magazine. In 1986, I finally convinced them to expand their travel coverage dramatically and offered to help with the long-range editorial planning. As a result, I went from being a strict freelancer to a contract employee. I became responsible for carpentering together an editorial travel calendar and for writing most of the stories. In exchange, they agreed to pay me an annual fee in 12 monthly instalments.*

That contract ended when the magazine was sold but by then I was the acknowledged expert in tennis travel and started my own Web site devoted to helping tennis vacationers make informed choices about where to go. Several national magazines continue to think of me when they need stories about tennis. All of this came about because I took that original advice and wrote about what I loved.

12

photography

In this chapter you will learn:
- camera options
- tips for getting good pics
- international photo manners.

Let's take a test. Look through the pages of a magazine. What one element catches your eye? The answer, of course, is photography. And in the same manner that these visuals capture *your* imagination, they appeal to the editor. Why? Because they interest his readers.

For this reason alone, it makes good business sense to think in terms of a story package (a manuscript accompanied by pictures). When you consider the axiom 'Great pictures can sell *just good* prose', it's wise to learn the camera craft.

Understanding photography

As a travel writer, there are two reasons to take photographs when on location. One is to illustrate the story. The other is to force you to look at the details of the destination.

'I do not let equipment get in the way of seeing,' says Russ Johnson, travel editor of Redband Broadcasting and creator of Web travel magazine, The Connected Traveler (www.connectedtraveler.com). 'Quite the opposite, I use a camera as an excuse for examining a subject more thoroughly. As a filmmaker I look at both pictures and stories in terms of wide shot, medium shot and closeup. I may not use them all, but at least I have explored their possibilities.'

Several steps are necessary to achieve *oneness* with the camera:

1 Select an easy-to-use, uncomplicated camera that will produce clear, sharp pictures. You don't want the mechanics of camera operation to impede your process of seeing and recording a locale or event.

2 Shoot a lot. Film is inexpensive, especially when compared to the cost and effort of recreating the trip. Expect no more than a 1:10 shooting ratio (one good photo for every ten shots).

3 Analyze your photographs to determine how to improve them. Is there a sense of design? Did you frame the subject? What about colour? Are the pictures slightly over- or underexposed? Should the subject face the centre rather than out of the frame? Look at the background and make necessary adjustments. (Is there a pile of rubbish in the background or a lamppost seemingly growing from the top of your subject's head?)

Camera selection

Your goal is to find a camera that makes you comfortable, but allows you to do a good job. With so many different models and brands from which to choose, buying a new camera can be a tougher decision than picking a vacation spot.

Your primary concern will probably be whether you want to purchase a single lens reflex (SLR) or a point-and-shoot. The SLR is a popular choice for the photojournalist for two reasons:

1 What you see in the viewfinder is exactly what will be recorded on film.
2 It has interchangeable lenses – lenses that offer innumerable creative possibilities.

An alternative to the SLR is the fully automatic camera with a non-interchangeable zoom lens. And while this camera offers the advantage of being only one piece of equipment to carry and very easy to operate, it does have artistic limitations. The digital camera is an additional option, which appeals to more travel writers as the print quality increases and the price decreases because you see the results immediately and it eliminates film issues (expense and airport security).

Camera equipment and extras

When you begin to equip your SLR camera, there are certain considerations to keep in mind. Examine your experience and your photography needs; then decide on lenses, filters and the like. Remember, gadgets only weigh you down.

24 mm lens
Extra wide-angle lens well suited to landscapes, architecture and areas with tight shooting space. The resulting pictures illustrate sweeping views.

28 mm – 105 mm zoom lens
Single lens that covers the spectrum of a wide-angle, a normal and a telephoto lens.

80 mm – 210 mm zoom lens
Telephoto lens that brings distant subjects closer.

Polarizing filter
Filter commonly used to eliminate unwanted reflections; it also saturates colour, creating dramatic contrasts; for example, snow-white foreground set against a deep blue sky.

UV (ultraviolet) filter
Used to protect the camera lens, as well as to cut haze.

Electronic flash
Flash is often necessary for indoor photography; it is surprisingly helpful for some outdoor pictures taken in bright sunlight (flash fills in dark shadows).

Cable release
Camera movement is avoided by using a cable release. It is essential when shooting a time exposure or at a slow shutter speed.

Disposable camera
An inexpensive option for some specialized photography needs (for instance, panoramic and underwater shots).

Nondescript photo bag
A small backpack or a padded duffel bag, as opposed to a distinctive camera bag, doesn't advertise that you are carrying expensive camera equipment.

In addition to all this, your camera should have a sturdy and comfortable shoulder strap.

Film facts

The three basic types of 35mm film are colour print, colour slide and black-and-white print film. I recommend using colour slide film for a variety of reasons:

1 Printers prefer colour slide film for making colour separations (separations must be made before a colour picture can be printed).
2 Colour prints can be made from colour slides.
3 Black and white prints can be made from colour slides with an internegative.

Colour slide film is the most versatile of film types.

Kodachrome 64 (or 25, a slower film), Fujichrome 50 and 100 are good choices for colour film. Another option, Fujichrome 400 colour slide film, allows you to shoot indoors, at twilight, on dark and rainy days – in low light level conditions. Kodak's Tri-X is the standard black and white choice for newspaper photographers.

Getting good photography

photography

12

Always cover the basics. An *overview* capturing the essence of the entire scene (usually shot from an elevated spot). *Group shots* of residents interacting (working, playing, praying and eating together). *Face shots* of individuals. *Workplaces* and *residences* showing how the city works; how its people live. *Noted landmarks* for editors who want their readers to capture an immediate sense of place. Another editor favourite is the *local in native dress* (e.g. businessman in Bermuda shorts and knee socks, a common sight in the capital city of Hamilton).

A good photograph is composed of many elements. The following box contains some tips that will help you create winning images.

Photo tips

Compose in the viewfinder. Envision what you see as a finished photograph.

Shoot tight shots. Get in twice as close to the subject as you would think. Leave room in some of your photographs for editors to crop. (Think in terms of a cover – allowing room at the top and bottom of the frame for the name of the publication, date, etc.)

Follow the rule of thirds. Within the viewfinder, draw two imaginary lines horizontally (dividing in equal thirds) and two vertically (dividing in equal thirds). Place the subject where these lines intersect. Rule: don't centre the subject.

Shoot horizontal and vertical shots. Shoot most subjects in both horizontal and vertical formats. Your eye for composition sometimes dictates: a horizontal shot might best depict a team of horses traversing a mountain path whereas Seattle's Space Needle seems a natural vertical shot.

Get people in shots. If at all possible, use people. And when there are no people, look for animals. Even a pristine landscape – like the shore at sunset – comes alive with the inclusion of a lone beachcomber wandering the surf's edge.

A person, an animal, even a boat or a tree helps create the concept of scale in a landscape – especially with a subject of mammoth proportions like an iceberg or waterfall.

Shoot people in their element. Think of people shots in terms of environmental portraits (where a person works or lives); show them performing an activity related to the article. In most cases, avoid posed shots with the subject looking directly into the camera. Sometimes, however, such portraits can be very strong and compelling. (*Note*: When a subject looks directly into the lens, always focus on his eyes.)

Look for details. Concentrate on capturing the specifics of a locale; whether it's a building's intricate woodwork, a rose in a young woman's hand or a local postage stamp.

Seek unusual angles. Look for natural frames and colourful objects to add interest and dimension (e.g. shoot a building through flowers in the foreground). Stand on a ladder or lie on the ground to get a different perspective. Place an object in the foreground to create a three-dimensional effect. When the subject is a well-known landmark, shoot it from a creative angle; then go for the normal, expected view.

Shoot at prime time. Most photographers favour early morning and evening light because the colours are stronger and there is unique peace at both daybreak and sunset. In addition, this timing makes it unnecessary to contend with severe shadows created by overhead sun. However, don't squander the artistic possibilities inclement weather provides – the magical sheen captured after a downpour of rain or the sense of surrealism depicted in a fog-bound landscape.

Aim to get red or yellow in shots. The inclusion of these brilliant colours brings the picture to life. Where do you find red and yellow? Usually in clothing. Imagine a yellow raincoat on a pedestrian scurrying across a street on a gray, rainy day.

Bracket your exposures. In addition to shooting the photograph at the exposure indicated by a light meter or the automatic reading on the camera, shoot a picture on each side of this reading. When using colour slide film, I will underexpose by about a half stop for richer colour saturation.

Use aperture/shutter speed priority for effect. Understand the creative application of both camera settings and employ them. (Guidelines for aperture/shutter applications will be detailed in your camera operating manual.)

Get clues from postcards and posters. Use each as a visual reference. Look at them and learn from them.

Photograph people *after* the interview. The best portraits come once a rapport has been established (assuming the interview goes well, of course).

Pursue one subject. Take photographs of one topic wherever you go; for example, front doors or buses or hats or grocery stores. Who knows, that series of pictures of dogs with their owners taken from around the world might be the basis for an article, even a coffee table book one day.

Know when to change film. If you are approaching a climatic situation where you expect to take a lot of pictures, put in a fresh roll of film. Don't chance *missing the action* because you're changing your film.

Mind your photo *manners*

Consider it a privilege to photograph someone, especially in a country that is not your homeland. Friendliness, honesty and good manners are the principles to follow when photographing people. Hence, heed the message when a potential subject turns his back on you or pulls a scarf over her face. The communique is 'don't take my picture'. Remember that it is smart to learn as much as you can about local laws and customs before taking pictures of people.

Let's face it, cameras are considered intrusive. Aware of this natural aversion, I sometimes use a telephoto lens to get candid shots. Some of my best people pictures from Athens were the result of this type of *undercover* photography – taken while seated at an outdoor café in the Plaka.

Is a photo release necessary?

When photographing people during your travels, it is certainly smart – but not always practical – to get the permission of those you are photographing. You have the right to take a picture of anybody who is in a public place; but only for editorial usage. So ask subjects to sign a release if you think there is any reason they would object to having their picture published in an editorial context.

This has never been a well-defined black or white issue but while there is a lack of general consensus from travel writers on exactly when a photo release is needed, on this they do agree: if you plan to sell a picture that may be used in an advertisement or as a cover, you must have a release signed.

Sample model release

Cynthia W. Dial
Writer/photographer
(Street address)
San Diego, CA 92130 USA
(telephone number)

Photography and editorial release

For consideration, receipt of which I hereby acknowledge, I hereby give ___(your name)___ the right and permission to copyright, publish, reproduce, resell or otherwise use my name, likeness, description and/or photographs and pictures of me, or in which I may be included, in whole or in part; for magazine or newspaper editorial publication, promotion, reproduction or other lawful purpose.

(Date)_____   (Name)_____

(Address)_____

(City & State) (Postal Code) (Country)

(Signature of model or guardian)
(Telephone)_____

Remember this is only one example of a model release. Some releases are more technically worded and complicated. Others are simple and straightforward, but may be equally effective in getting a layperson's signature because they are less intimidating. It is important to note that some publications may require you to use their release form before accepting your material.

Also be aware that parental consent is always required for minors (legal age varies in different parts of the world).

Solutions for the non-photographer

For those of you aspiring travel writers who do not consider yourselves adequate photographers, there are options.

One of those options is to align yourself with a good, intuitive photographer. The downside of this partnership is a logistical one because it requires travel arrangements for two rather than one, making a request for free or subsidized travel more difficult.

Other alternatives may be more practical and are usually free of charge. Because national tourist offices, governmental agencies and chambers of commerce want to showcase their particular area, they will eagerly share photography with travel journalists.

Sometimes a hotel, restaurant or tourist attraction will have its own photography file and be able to assist with your visual needs. And if your story touches a business or organization that will benefit from publicity, its public relations department may be willing to help. The final solution involves a price – the purchase of stock photos from a photo library.

How to submit photography

- Submit mounted colour slides in clear plastic sleeves.
- Black and white photography submissions should be 5″ × 7″ or 8″ × 10″ prints (never 3″ × 5″).
- Always identify slides and prints with your name, address and telephone number.
- Include captions with your photography. In a simple sentence tell where, when and what's going on. Identify people when you can. (Attach the caption to the back of prints; number slides and coordinate your caption sheet accordingly.)
- Unless stipulated otherwise, it is standard for photos to be sold on a one-time rights basis. Notate this specification on the caption sheet by writing 'All photos sold on a one-time rights basis' to eliminate the potential for any misunderstanding.
- Never submit originals, unless a publication specifies. In this case, send them insured, registered, request a return receipt and include an SASE (SAE).
- When submitting to several newspapers, enclose an SAP for the editor to return – indicating his preference for black and white prints or colour slides. This inclusion can represent a tremendous savings in reprint costs.

13

press trips and independent itineraries

In this chapter you will learn:
- how to ask for free travel benefits
- tips from a PR professional
- the freebie conflict of interest issue.

One of the most frequently asked questions in my travel writing class involves free, or as I like to say, *subsidized* travel. Someone has to explore the streets of Tokyo and write about the experience; it might as well be you. Right?

But as you've hopefully culled from previous chapters of this book, travel writing is a business. And as expected in most businesses, the necessary steps you must take to receive industry benefits are professional ones.

Advice to the beginner

My initial advice to the beginner when seeking sponsors for a trip is to *ask the right way*. Never make demands (you'd be amazed how many travel writers do just that).

Before you approach an airline, a cruise line, a hotel, a tourist bureau or a public relations firm, think about your project. Whether you make this contact by letter or telephone, be prepared to communicate your story idea in one to two sentences because anything longer suggests that either you or your topic are unfocused.

If you choose to submit by mail (which I would suggest to the beginner), prepare a proposal. It is more than likely that you'll be requested to provide this information even if the potential sponsor expresses interest during a phone conversation.

This proposal should include a cover letter telling about you, particulars of the project and a mention of a letter of assignment (if you have one). Describe your exact request; the more details the better. The verbiage should be clear and straightforward: 'I would like to request accommodation at your resort for a portion of the time I will be in Acapulco. I expect to be there July 12 to July 18, 2002.'

Additional proposal inclusions should be your bio (tailored for each sponsor), clips of relevant and recent work and, as always, a business card.

I know the reaping of travel benefits is alluring, but good guidance might be to pay your own way in the beginning. Concentrate on the *cake* (the destination) not the *icing* (the freebies). Simply focus on your end goal: getting published. Query continually, research thoroughly, submit your best writing and you will accumulate clip after clip. Then once

Use the common sense approach

1 Approach every sponsor in a polite, professional manner. And accept a *no* in an equally gracious fashion.

2 To get your very first invitation, cultivate contacts, e.g. PR firms specializing in travel clients, organizations geared to certain areas of the world like Pacific Asia Travel Association (PATA).

3 Don't request space during major holidays or events (e.g. Christmas in the Holy Land, Carnival in Rio de Janeiro or Super Bowl) unless it is critical to your piece.

4 Follow up with a telephone call a couple of days after sending a written proposal to a potential sponsor.

5 Always send thank you notes and copies of published stories to host(s), airline, CVB, etc.

you're established as a serious travel writer, you will turn down more travel invitations than you will ever be able to accept. I promise.

Press trips

A press trip is arranged for a group of writers to familiarize them with the destination, the mode of transportation or an event taking place in order that they may write about it. Press trips give writers an overview – they are a great way to do research quickly. Usually most expenses are paid, including food and beverage, accommodation, airfare and admission fees. Because you are with other writers, press trips create tremendous networking opportunities.

The downside to press trips is that there is little free time to explore individual interests or to conduct specific interviews.

Public relations specialist Kate Stingley addresses her firm's standard policy on press trips:

Freelance writers must be qualified and reputable, with outlets that are compatible to our clients' goals. And they must be willing to supply recent clips of related stories. We also consider journalists who have been referred by other writers with whom we have worked and/or other PR companies we trust that have the same standards as we do.

Staff members are slightly different as they already have an outlet, but the story must be assigned (not a research trip or a look-see). Individual visits are treated a little differently as the time and expense involved is considerably less.

Have a look at the tips in the following box, too.

Public relations' expectations

Kate Stingley is a public relations specialist with a New York City boutique firm that specializes in unique destinations, luxury hotels and resorts. Collected from 11 years of experience, here are some insider's tips:

As a sponsor, a public relations firm expects the travel writer to:

- *Be a good guest – not demanding, nor expecting everything to be complimentary – and be respectful of our hosts and other group members.*

- *Have a mature understanding that sometimes things change, e.g. an itinerary may be slightly different, some activities might run longer than originally planned, it might rain, sites may be closed, the upgrade from coach does not come through and so on.*

- *Diligently pursue story placement(s) in a timely manner.*

- *Ask intelligent questions and be as certain as possible that the host is aware of any specific needs relating to the assignment prior to the trip. (The same is true for other needs, e.g. health considerations, food preferences, etc.)*

As a resource, a public relations firm provides the writer with:

- *Clear-cut expectations – no ambiguity.*

- *An itinerary of events/activities based on the focus of the trip. (We always try to build in some free time for individual pursuits so that all the stories are not the same.)*

- *A specific list of what we provide such as lodging, airfare, access to various itinerary items, meals, etc. Equally important are the specifics of what we do not cover, e.g. phone, minibar, additional spa treatments, meals (if not specified), etc.*

Independent itineraries

Just as its name indicates, an independent itinerary gives the travel writer *independence*. You are not travelling with a group to a pre-set itinerary; you set the itinerary and see only what you want to see.

Obtaining subsidies for this type of travel, however, requires more effort on your part. It calls for the development of a day-by-day plan of where and when you want to go and what you want to see. And once you've created the master plan, you must contact individual hotels, attractions and airlines (if applicable) about complimentary travel arrangements or admissions.

Tourist boards/CVBs can be tremendous allies in this effort. The benefit of working with them is that their goal is to promote their country and they can make key connections for you.

Policy on sponsored trips

Because it is considered a conflict of interest, some publications will not accept submissions from writers who have accepted any kind of free travel. Do your homework in advance and know a publication's *subsidized travel* policy before submitting a piece written from a fully or partially sponsored trip. To avoid potential problems in this area, make it your policy to accept invitations for free trips only when there's a certainty of story placement.

The best situation, of course, is to accept the offer of a *free* hotel stay, for example, after you've written and published your story. Many sponsors are delighted to make this offer to a proven journalist.

Words of writing wisdom

... from the convention and visitors bureau (CVB)

Charles Leong, a travel and tourism veteran for some 30 years, is Senior Director Tourism Business at the Singapore Tourism Board's head office in Singapore.

Consider the following before approaching a CVB:

- *Writers who have an assignment(s) are more likely to receive wider assistance like land arrangements at the destination, interviews with relevant people, and at times, even transportation to/from that country. So it would be beneficial for writers to show proof of assignments(s) when approaching CVBs for help.*

- *Maintain a portfolio of all articles that were published. This is useful as a performance indicator of writers' work and style.*

- *The less demanding the writer, the more willing is the CVB to help and go the extra mile in arrangements within the destination. Hence, writers must be realistic in their expectations of a CVB's level of facilitation.*

- *It is very important for writers to provide copies of the published articles to the CVBs as soon as available. This enhances the professionalism and credibility of the writers and strengthens their relationship with the CVB. Moreover, this enables the CVB to assess its return on investment. More importantly for writers, the CVB would be able to give good referrals when asked by other CVBs.*

14

keeping records, et al

In this chapter you will learn:
- the importance of detailed records
- about deductable expenses
- some financial tips from a pro.

There are basically two principal reasons to keep financial records:

1 to track your costs per project
2 for tax purposes.

Personally, I have never had the mental fortitude to tally my hourly/monthly rate, but as a US citizen, I keep records for the Internal Revenue Service (IRS).

Record-keeping basics

The principles are simple: keep track of every travel-related expense. (See the following boxes for potentially deductible travel expenditures.) Note that sanctioned travel expenses vary from country to country, depending on individual laws. Thus, it is always recommended to consult an accounting specialist regarding financial issues. See Words of wisdom at the end of this chapter.

Pre-travel expenses

- vaccinations
- trip-related insurance (e.g. trip interruption, trip cancellation, overseas medical, camera and baggage, rental car, accident, etc.)
- film, batteries and audio tapes
- research books (guidebooks, general destination books, etc.)
- maps
- luggage.

On-the-road expenses

- ground transportation to/from home (shuttle, taxi, car mileage, etc.)
- transportation to/from destination (air, ship, train, etc.)
- hotel accommodation
- food and drink (snack at airport, coffee, lunches, dinners, cocktails, etc.) for yourself and for anyone you interview
- admission to attractions, theatres, museums, parks, etc
- lessons and equipment rental (e.g. surfing, skiing, snow-mobiling)

- departure taxes/surcharges
- tips (baggage handling, taxi, doorman, etc.)
- magazines, postcards, books (research materials)
- film processing and developing
- childcare expenses.

At-home expenses

- at-home office
- office furniture
- office supplies
- office phone, fax and Internet expenses
- computer equipment, software and repairs
- photocopy machine and services
- camera equipment and supplies
- recording equipment
- automobile expenses and parking (keep automobile log in your car) or public transportation
- business lunches or dinners/at-home entertainment costs (for business associates)
- fees (attorney and accounting) and dues (professional organizations)
- registration fees (conferences, seminars)
- classes (writing, creative, grammar, etc.)
- advertising and promotion
- letterhead, envelopes, business cards, mailing labels, etc
- postage and courier
- expenses for designing and maintaining a website.

Copy protection

Although there is no worldwide standard with respect to tax laws and valid tax deductions, it is nevertheless wise to keep copies of manuscripts, dated query letters, letters of acceptance and rejection and any business-related correspondence (CVBs, magazines, newspapers, airlines, etc.). If and when it is necessary to prove legitimacy as a working travel writer, all this documentation will assist in that endeavour.

Words of writing wisdom

... about your financial records

Richard C. Waters, CPA, is president of noted accounting firm Waters, Hardy and Company, P. C. located in Dallas, Texas.

Any travel claimed as a business expense has to have an underlying business activity associated with it. Travel writing is in itself a business activity, but there has to be a profit motive behind the business activity in order to avoid it appearing as a hobby.

A good rule of thumb is to be able to show a business profit in three out of five years. Not all writers are able to do this. Breaking into the industry is very difficult and can take a long time. Therefore, the above-referenced rule of thumb is not necessarily applicable to all businesses, namely the travel writing profession.

One way to demonstrate that the travelling you are doing is a business is to maintain good records of your expenses. Receipts with the proper documentation is always a way to show tax authorities that the travel is related to a genuine business endeavour.

In addition, make sure that you keep records showing the number of articles you submit for publishing. Not all the articles will be published, but demonstrating the amount of work you generate will help to show your travelling is not a hobby.

Words of writing wisdom

... to conclude

Let's end with words of wisdom I've always found compelling in the premise of Anne Lamott's bestseller *Bird by Bird*. She drew inspiration from a 30-year-old incident involving her brother who was ten at the time. He was trying to begin writing a report on birds that he'd had three months to complete; it was due the next day. Close to tears, he sat at the kitchen table surrounded by binder paper, pencils and unopened books on birds – he was immobilized by the enormity of the task. Lamott's father sat down beside his son, put his arm around the boy's shoulder and said: 'Bird by bird, buddy. Just take it bird by bird.'

A parting thought: If you want to be a travel writer, *write*.

glossary

advertorial Advertising written to resemble editorial material. It is paid for by an advertiser and the word 'advertisement' appears with the piece.

AR Abbreviation for all rights. Writer sells the right to use the material anywhere and forever; sells the copyright.

B&W Abbreviation for black and white photographs.

bimonthly Every two months.

biweekly Every two weeks.

byline Name of the author appearing with the published piece.

circulation The distribution of a publication.

clips Samples of your published work.

column inch Type within a one-inch measurement of a typeset column.

contract A legally binding, signed document between two parties establishing mutually agreeable terms.

copyediting Editing a manuscript for grammar, punctuation and printing style but not for subject content.

copyright Protection of an author's written work.

cover letter A brief letter of introduction accompanying a finished manuscript. (This is not a query letter.)

CV Curriculum Vitae. A brief account of one's education, qualifications, and previous occupations. Also referred to as **résumé**.

disk A magnetic plate on which computer data are stored.

dot-matrix Printed type where individual characters are composed by a pattern of tiny dots. Near letter quality (NLQ) dot-matrix submissions are generally acceptable to editors.

evergreen   An article which is timeless like 'History of America's 4th of July Celebration'.

fair use   Short passages from copyrighted material may be used without infringement of the author's rights.

first person   An article written from the author's viewpoint.

FNASR   First North American serial rights. Writer sells a publication the right to publish an article for the first time in North America. Unless otherwise specified, copyright reverts to the author after publication.

freelance writer   A writer who is not exclusively affiliated with a publication, who has the right to write for a variety of publications.

genre   Refers to a classification of writing, such as mystery, romance, science fiction or travel writing.

hard copy   A physical copy (as opposed to electronic transmission) of the manuscript.

hook   Element of an article that attracts attention or entices.

IRC   International Reply Coupon. Postage for use on reply mail in countries other than your own.

kill fee   Fee for a completed article which was assigned but subsequently cancelled.

lead   The opening paragraph of a story.

Lead time   The time between an editor's receipt of an article and its actual publication.

masthead   A box or column, usually on the editorial page of a newspaper or magazine, giving the names and positions of the editorial staff.

model release   Signed permission giving the right to use a photograph for publication. (The release is signed by a guardian if the subject is a juvenile.)

monthly   Publication that comes out once a month.

ms   Abbreviation for manuscript.

mss   Abbreviation for manuscripts.

multiple submission   Several magazines are sent the same article at the same time. Also called simultaneous submission.

NLQ   Abbreviation for near letter-quality print, a degree of print quality that is required by some editors for computer printout submissions.

NTO   National Tourist Organization, a nation's government tourist association.

on assignment   A writer is travelling and working on a pre-assigned story.

on spec   Abbreviation for on speculation. An editor agrees to consider an article upon its submission but is under no obligation to buy the finished piece.

one-time rights   Publication buys the right to print an article or photograph on a one-time basis.

peg   Aspect of an article that relates it to a date or an event.

POA   Payment on acceptance. Payment is sent to a writer when the piece is accepted, before publication.

POP   Payment on publication. Payment is sent to a writer after the piece is published.

press kit   A comprehensive collection of materials like brochures, booklets, press releases, a facts sheet, maps and photographs compiled on a single subject like a country, hotel or historic site. Also called a media kit.

press release   A news story prepared and distributed by a public relations firm, a communications department or a governmental agency.

pseudonym   Also called pen name. The use of a name other than your legal name as your byline on articles, stories or books.

quarterly   Publication distributed fours times annually.

query letter   Letter to an editor proposing a story idea.

regional publication   Magazine or newspaper with a limited distribution area.

rejection   Letter from the editor stating the manuscript or query does not meet the publication's needs.

reprint rights   See **second serial rights**

résumé   See **CV**

roundup   Article including a number of like subjects on a single theme, for example '18th Century Pubs in London' or 'California Golf Resorts.'

SAE   Abbreviation for stamped addressed envelope. Should always be included with correspondence to an editor. Also referred to as **SASE** (self-addressed stamped envelope).

SAP   Abbreviation for stamped addressed postcard. Is sometimes sent in lieu of **SAE**.

SASE   See **SAE**

sample copy   Copy of a publication sent by the editor upon request. There may be a charge. An SAE should be included.

second serial rights   Also called reprint rights. A writer sells a publication the right to reprint material that has appeared elsewhere.

semi-monthly   Twice a month.

semi-weekly   Twice a week.

sidebar   A small column presented as a companion to the article, with useful data about airlines, weather, passport information, etc. or specific information on one aspect of the story.

simultaneous rights   Sale of the same article at the same time to more than one publication in non-competing circulation areas.

slant   The style or approach of a story so that it fits with the specific needs of the publication and appeals to its readers.

STO   State tourist organization, the tourist association for individual states.

tear sheet   Pages from a magazine or newspaper containing your published article.

unsolicited manuscript   An article that was not requested by an editor.

word processor   A computer program, used in lieu of a typewriter.

writer's guidelines   A detailed summary of exactly what an editor wants in a submitted piece. While they vary, many contain precise information about content, word count, photographic requirements, formatting, editorial preferences, pay and pay schedule. Also called author's guidelines.

references

The public library

Encyclopedia of Associations (US)
Encyclopedia of Associations – International Organizations
   (Australia, Canada, UK and others)
Gale Directory of Publications & Broadcast Media (US)
International Literary Market Place (Australia and UK
   primarily)
International Writers' & Artists' Yearbook (Australia,
   Canada, UK and US primarily)*
Literary Market Place (Canada and US)
New York Times Index
Reader's Guide to Periodical Literature
Times of London Index
Ulrich's International Periodicals Directory
Who's Who (regional, subject, international)
Working Press of the Nation (US)
World Chamber of Commerce Directory
*Writer's Guide to Book Editors, Publishers and Literary
   Agents* (Canada and US)*
Writer's Market (Canada and US)*
Yearbook of International Organizations

* Also found in bookstores.

The travel writer's library

Almanacs (*Information Please, People's* and *World Almanac*)
Bartlett's Familiar Quotations
The Cambridge Factfinder
Chase's Calendar of Annual Events
A Dictionary of Geology
The Facts on File Visual Dictionary
Facts on File: A Weekly World News Digest
Find It Fast: How to Uncover Expert Information on Any Subject
The Guinness Book of World Records
Larousse Gastronomique
The Little Brown Book of Anecdotes
The New York Public Library Desk Reference
Oxford Dictionary of Foreign Words and Phrases
The Penguin Rhyming Dictionary
Photographer's Market
Simpson's Contemporary Quotations
The Timetables of History
Webster's New Geographical Dictionary
Worldwide Multilingual Phrase Book: Survival Skills for Over 40 Languages

Web sites for worldwide tourist offices

Antigua and Barbuda Department of Tourism
www.antigua-barbuda.org

Aruba Tourism Authority
www.aruba.com

Australia Tourist Commission
www.aussie.net.au

Austrian National Tourist Office
www.austria-tourism.at/us

Bahamas Tourism
www.bahamas.com

Belgian Tourist Office
www.visitbelgium.com

British Tourist Authority
www.travelbritain.org

British Virgin Islands Tourist Board
www.bviwelcome.com

California Office of Tourism
www.gocalif.com

Canadian Tourism Commission
www.canadatourism.com

Cancun Convention and Visitors' Bureau
www.gocancun.com

Cayman Islands Tourism
www.caymanislands.ky

China National Tourist Office
www.cnto.org

Curacao Convention Bureau
www.curacao-tourism.com

Dominican Republic Tourism
www.dominicana.com.do

Egyptian Tourist Office
www.interoz.com/egypt

French Government Tourist Office
www.francetourism.com

German National Tourist Office
www.visits-to-germany.com

Hong Kong Tourism Board
www.hkta.org

Government of India Tourist Office
www.tourindia.com

Irish Tourist Board
www.shamrock.org

Israel Government Tourist Office
www.goisrael.com

Italian Government Tourist Office
www.italiantourism.com

Jamaica Tourist Board
www.jamaicatravel.com

Japan National Tourist Organization
www.japantravelinfo.com

Korea National Tourism Organization
www.tour2Korea.com

Las Vegas Convention and Visitors Authority
www.lasvegas24hours.com

Malaysia Tourism Promotion Board
www.tourismmalaysia.com

Mexico Tourism Boad
www.visitmexico.com

Netherlands Board of Tourism
www.goholland.com

New York Convention and Visitors Bureau
www.nycvisit.com

New Zealand Tourism
www.purenz.com

Portuguese National Tourist Office
www.portugalinsite.pt

Puerto Rico Convention Bureau
www.meetpuertorico.com

Russian National Tourist Office
www.russia-travel.com

St Maarten Tourist Bureau
www.st-maarten.com

St Martin Tourist Office
www.st-martin.org

Scandinavian Tourist Board
(Denmark, Finland, Iceland, Norway and Sweden)
www.goscandinavia.com

Singapore Tourist Promotion Board
www.tourismsingapore.com

South African Tourism
www.southafrica.net

Tourist Office of Spain
www.okspain.org

Switzerland Tourism
www.MySwitzerland.com

Tahiti Tourisme
www.gotahiti.com

Tourism Authority Thailand
www.tourismthailand.org

Turkish Government Tourist Office
www.turkey.org/turkey

Turks and Caicos Tourist Board
www.tourismturkey.org

English language newspaper websites

The Boston Herald
www.bostonherald.com

Evening Times (Glasgow, Scotland)
www.eveningtimes.co.uk

Hong Kong Standard
www.hkstandard.com

Honolulu Star Bulletin
www.honolulustarbulletin.com

The Irish Times
www.irishtimes.com

The Japan Times
www.japantimes.co.jp

The Jerusalem Post
www.jpost.com

Los Angeles Times
www.latimes.com

The Miami Herald
www.miamiherald.com

Montreal Gazette
www.montrealgazette.com

The News (Mexico City)
www.thenewsmexico.com

New York Times
www.nytimes.com

San Diego Union-Tribune
www.uniontrib.com

San Francisco Chronicle
www.sfgate.com/chronicle

South China Morning Post (Hong Kong)
www.SCMP.com

The Straits Times (Singapore)
www.straitstimes.asia1.com.sg/home

Sydney Morning Herald
www.smh.com.au

Times of London
www.londontimes.com

Toronto Star
www.torontostar.com

Vancouver Sun
www.vancouversun.com

Washington Post
www.washingtonpost.com

The publisher has used its best endeavours to ensure that the URLs for external websites referred to in this book are correct and active at the time of going to press. However, the publisher has no responsibility for the websites and can make no guarantee that a site will remain live or that the content is or will remain appropriate.

index

teach
yourself

writing a novel
nigel watts

- Do you want to turn your ideas into a finished novel?
- Do you need to overcome writer's block?
- Are you looking for advice on getting published?

Writing A Novel takes you through the whole process of writing a novel, from the germ of an idea, through developing plot, character and theme, to preparing it for publication. This fascinating analysis of novel writing will appeal to both new and experienced authors, whether you work through it as you write or dip into it as you go along.

"This should be a very useful book for those aspiring writers to whom its is addressed."
PD James

Nigel Watts, taught creative writing from 1989, the year in which he published his first novel, *The Life Game*. He went on to publish three more novels as well as children's fiction.

teach
yourself

creative writing
dianne doubtfire

- Do you want to know more about the writing process?
- Are you eager to develop your talent and improve your skills?
- Do you want to find out about the industry and getting published?

Creative Writing is the ideal practical handbook for any aspiring author. Using exercises to explore topics, it will encourage you to develop, direct and edit your creative ideas in addition to giving you invaluable guidance on how to present work for publication.

The late **Dianne Doubtfire** was a successful author of both fiction and non-fiction. This edition has been fully revised and expanded by **Ian Burton,** a former pupil of Dianne's and a published author and lecturer in creative writing.

teach
yourself

better handwriting

rosemary sassoon & gunnlaugur se briem

- Do you want to improve your handwriting technique?
- Do you experience problems with writing and want help?
- Are you looking to experiment and develop your own style.

Better Handwriting is a practical and informative guide. The way we write mirrors our mood and character. It is the way we project ourselves to the world – and other people often judge us by our handwriting. This book is specifically written for adults and will help you to improve and develop a mature and individual style.

Rosemary Sassoon is a letterform consultant specializing in the educational and medical aspects of handwriting. She has a PhD from Reading University. **Gunnlaugur SE Briem** is an Icelandic designer and has a PhD from the Royal College of Art in London.